NEW WAYS TO
Appliqué™

Edited by Jeanne Stauffer & Sandra L. Hatch

HOUSE of
WHITE
BIRCHES
PUBLISHERS
SINCE 1947

New Ways to Applique

Editors: Jeanne Stauffer, Sandra L. Hatch
Associate Editor: Dianne Schmidt
Copy Editors: Michelle Beck, Sue Harvey, Nicki Lehman, Linda Rulka

Photography: Tammy Christian, Kelly Heydinger, Christena Green
Photography Stylist: Tammy Nussbaum

Publishing Services Manager: Brenda Gallmeyer
Art Director: Brad Snow
Book Design: Jessi Butler
Cover Design: Brad Snow
Technical Artist: Connie Rand
Graphic Artists: Jessi Butler, Ronda Bechinski
Production Assistants: Janet Bowers, Marj Morgan
Traffic Coordinator: Sandra Beres

Chief Executive Officer: John Robinson
Publishing Director: David McKee
Book Marketing Manager: Craig Scott
Editorial Director: Vivian Rothe
Publishing Services Manager: Brenda Wendling

Printed in the United States of America
First Printing: 2003
Library of Congress Number: 2002113548
ISBN: 1-59217-013-7

Quilt Note

If you love to appliqué, you will love this book. If you do not already love to appliqué, you will soon! When you try the new products and techniques featured, you'll find appliqué easier and more fun than ever before!

We asked quilt designers to send us projects that illustrate the techniques they use for making appliqué quilts that are much quicker to complete and easy enough for beginning quilters. We also requested that manufacturers send us the latest available products and tools that make appliqué fun for everyone. See page 176 for a contact list for these products.

Of course, a product or technique that is "new" to one quilter may not be "new" to the next quilter, but we think even the most experienced among you will find some new techniques or products to try. Some of the techniques/products we introduce are best used for specific situations: for example, we might feature a product that aids in multiple-layer appliqué. Other techniques can be used for almost any appliqué pattern. We know there are many ways to stitch down an appliqué design.

We realize that not everyone has tried all the old, familiar methods for appliqué, so we included designs that demonstrate many of these techniques as well so this book will include as many different appliqué techniques and products as possible.

Some quilters tend to use the same method every time they appliqué, and you can do that with these designs. They are so fantastic that you'll want to make every quilt in the book! So what are you waiting for? It's time to appliqué!

Happy stitching,

Jeanne Stauffer   Sandra L. Hatch

Contents

Lullaby & Good Night

Home for Christmas

Picture Perfect

Cozy Comforts

Lullaby & Good Night

Patchwork Posies

By Judith Sandstrom

Three-dimensional flowers bloom on this combination appliqué-and-patchwork quilt.

3-D Appliqué

Simple stitch-and-turn flowers and leaves create 3-D shapes. Double-fold bias tape is used for the stems, which are applied with ¼"-wide HeatnBond The Quilter's Edge Lite iron-on adhesive by Therm O Web.

Nine-Patch
7½" x 7½" Block

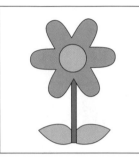

Posy
7½" x 7½" Block

Project Specifications

Skill Level: Beginner
Quilt Size: 42½" x 62½"
Block Size: 7½" x 7½"
Number of Blocks: 17

Materials

- ½ yard each rose, blue and yellow tone-on-tones
- ⅝ yard navy solid
- ⅝ yard lavender tone-on-tone
- ¾ yard green print
- 1½ yards white-on-white print
- Thin batting 49" x 69"
- Backing 49" x 69"
- All-purpose thread to match fabrics
- White hand-quilting thread
- 1 package Wrights green double-fold bias tape
- ½ yard HeatnBond Lite iron-on adhesive
- 1¾ yards ¼"-wide HeatnBond The Quilter's Edge Lite iron-on adhesive
- Basic sewing tools and supplies

Patchwork Posies
Placement Diagram
42½" x 62½"

Making Posy Blocks

Step 1. Prewash and iron all fabrics before cutting.

Step 2. Cut three 8" by fabric width strips white-on-white print; subcut into 8" squares for appliqué background. You will need 13 squares. Fold and crease each square to find the center.

Step 3. Cut three 3" by fabric width strips each rose, blue, yellow and lavender tone-on-tones; set aside for pieced borders.

Step 4. Fold each of the remaining rose, blue, yellow and lavender fabrics in half with right sides together.

Step 5. Prepare templates using pattern pieces given. Trace around the flower pattern piece on the wrong side of the layered fabric to make five lavender and four each rose, blue and yellow double-layer flowers, leaving ½" between traced lines.

Step 6. Cut a 1" slit in the center of one layer of each traced flower; pin layers together.

Step 7. Stitch on the marked line around each pinned flower shape as shown in Figure 1.

Figure 1
Stitch on the marked line around
each pinned flower shape.

Step 8. Cut out flower shapes ⅛"–¼" outside the stitched lines as shown in Figure 2; clip curves and indented points as shown in Figure 3.

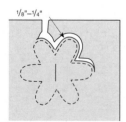

Figure 2
Cut out flower shapes ⅛"–¼"
outside the stitched lines.

Figure 3
Clip curves and
indented points.

Step 9. Turn shapes right side out through slits; smooth curves and indents and press flat.

Step 10. Trace and complete 17 flower centers

and 26 leaves from green print as in Steps 4–9 for making flowers, cutting a ¾" slit in each flower center and leaving the straight end of each leaf unstitched for turning.

Step 11. Cut thirteen 4½" pieces each green double-fold bias tape and ¼"-wide iron-on adhesive.

Step 12. Unfold one edge of each piece of bias tape; fold under raw end ¼" as shown in Figure 4. Refold on original lines. Iron a piece of ¼"-wide iron-on adhesive to the wrong side of each piece; remove paper backing.

Figure 4
Unfold 1 end of each piece of bias
tape; fold under raw edge ¼".

Step 13. Trace 34 flower center circles onto the paper side of the iron-on adhesive; cut out on traced lines.

Step 14. Fuse one iron-on adhesive circle over the slit cut in each fabric flower center. Repeat on the slit side of each fabric flower.

Step 15. Remove the paper circle from the fabric flower center and center on the unfused side of the flowers; fuse in place.

Step 16. Pin two leaves with raw edges overlapping each other 1" from the bottom edge and approximately 2½" from each side edge of a background square, using center creases as guides.

Step 17. Center one piece of bias tape over the leaves with the finished edge ⅞" from the bottom edge of the square as shown in Figure 5; fuse in place.

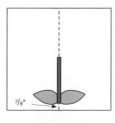

Figure 5
Center 1 piece of bias tape over the
leaves with the finished edge ⅞"
from the bottom edge of the square.

Step 18. Using all-purpose thread to match bias

tape, machine-stitch close to the edge on both sides and across the bottom of the bias tape.

Step 19. Remove the paper circle from the wrong side of each flower shape.

Step 20. Center a flower over the bias tape stem approximately 1" from the top edge of the block; remove paper backing from the backside and fuse in place.

Step 21. Machine-stitch around flower center to hold in place as in Step 18 to complete one block; repeat for 13 blocks.

Step 22. Cut four 5½" x 5½" squares white-on-white print for A. Referring to Figure 6, center a flower motif on each A square and stitch in place as in Step 20; repeat for four A squares.

Figure 6
Center a flower motif
on an A square.

Quilt Top Construction

Step 1. Cut seven 3" by fabric width strips each navy solid and white-on-white print. Subcut two white-on-white print strips into 3" square segments for B; you will need 24 B squares.

Step 2. Sew a white-on-white print strip between two navy solid strips with right sides together along length to make a C strip set; press seams toward navy solid strips. Repeat for three C strip sets.

Step 3. Sew a navy solid strip between two white-on-white print strips with right sides together along length to make a D strip set; press seams toward navy solid strips.

Step 4. Subcut C and D strip sets into 3" segments as shown in Figure 7. You will need 40 C and four D units.

Figure 7
Subcut C and
D strip sets into
3" segments.

Step 5. Join three Posy blocks with four C units to make an X row as shown in Figure 8; press seams toward blocks. Repeat for three X rows referring to the Placement Diagram for positioning of flowers.

Figure 8
Join 3 Posy blocks with 4 C
units to make an X row.

Step 6. Join one D and two C units to complete a Nine-Patch block as shown in Figure 9; repeat for four Nine-Patch blocks. Press seams in one direction.

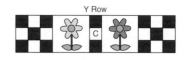

Figure 9
Join 1 D and 2 C
units to complete a
Nine-Patch block.

Figure 10
Join 2 Posy blocks with 2
Nine-Patch blocks and 1 C
unit to complete a Y row.

Step 7. Join two Posy blocks with two Nine-Patch blocks and one C unit to complete a Y row as shown in Figure 10; repeat for two Y rows referring to the Placement Diagram for positioning of flowers. Press seams toward blocks.

Step 8. Join four B squares with three C units to complete a sashing row as shown in Figure 11; repeat for six sashing rows. Press seams away from B.

Figure 11
Join 4 B squares with 3 C units
to complete a sashing row.

Step 9. Referring to Figure 12, join the X and Y rows with the sashing rows to complete the pieced center; press seams open.

Step 10. Using the strips cut in Step 3 of Making Posy Blocks, sew one strip of each fabric with right sides together

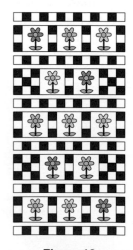

Figure 12
Join the X and Y rows with
the sashing rows to complete
the pieced center.

along length to make a strip set as shown in Figure 13; repeat for three strip sets.

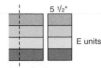

Figure 13
Subcut the strip sets into 5½" segments to make E units.

Step 11. Subcut the strip sets into 5½" segments to make E units, again referring to Figure 13; you will need 20 E units.

Step 12. Join six E units, removing segments from ends as shown in Figure 14 to make a side border strip; press seams in one direction. Repeat for two side border strips. Sew a strip to opposite long sides of the completed center referring to the Placement Diagram for positioning of strips; press seams toward strips.

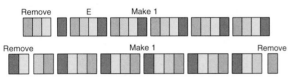

Figure 14
Join E units to make side border strips.

Step 13. Join four E units, removing segments from ends as shown in Figure 15 to make a top border strip; repeat for bottom border strip, again referring to Figure 15. Press seams in one direction. Sew an A square to each end of each strip referring to the Placement Diagram for positioning of flowers. Sew the strips to the top and bottom of the completed center referring to the Placement Diagram to complete the top; press seams toward strips.

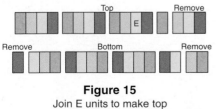

Figure 15
Join E units to make top and bottom border strips.

Finishing the Quilt

Step 1. Sandwich batting between the completed top and prepared backing piece; pin or baste layers together to hold flat for quilting.

Step 2. Quilt as desired by hand or machine. *Note: The quilt shown was hand-quilted ¼" from seams in all Posy blocks and ¼" from border seam using white hand-quilting thread.*

Step 3. When quilting is complete, trim batting and backing even with quilted top; remove pins or basting.

Step 4. Cut six 2¼" by fabric width strips green print. Join strips on short ends to make one long strip for binding.

Step 5. Fold the binding strip in half along length with wrong sides together; press.

Step 6. Bind edges to finish. ❖

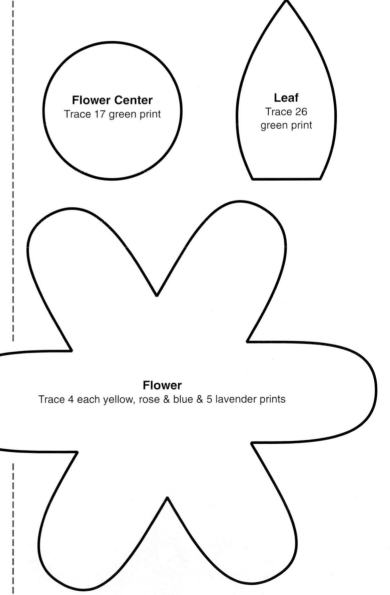

Flower Center
Trace 17 green print

Leaf
Trace 26
green print

Flower
Trace 4 each yellow, rose & blue & 5 lavender prints

Raggy Rainbow

By Lucy A. Fazely & Michael L. Burns

Ragged flannel strips create the soft, flowing curves of this rainbow-colored quilt.

Raggy Fringe Appliqué

Fabric strips are adhered to background fabric liquid fusible web and machine-stitching. Each strip is clipped along the curved edges. The ragged look is created when the quilt is washed and dried.

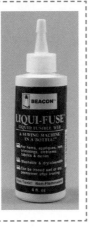

Raggy Rainbow
12" x 12" Block

Project Specifications
Skill Level: Beginner
Quilt Size: 72" x 84"
Block Size: 12" x 12"
Number of Blocks: 30

Materials
- ⅝ yard orange mottled flannel
- ⅔ yard yellow mottled flannel
- ¾ yard green mottled flannel
- ⅞ yard medium blue mottled flannel
- 1 yard dark blue mottled flannel
- 1⅛ yards light purple mottled flannel
- 2⅜ yards red mottled flannel
- 3⅝ yards light blue mottled flannel
- Batting 78" x 90"
- Backing 78" x 90"
- Red and blue all-purpose thread
- Rainbow variegated quilting and craft thread
- Clear nylon monofilament
- Beacon's Liqui-Fuse liquid fusible web
- Basic sewing tools and supplies

Raggy Rainbow
Placement Diagram
72" x 84"

Instructions

Step 1. Prepare templates using patterns given. Note that the curved edges of each piece do not require any seam allowance.

Step 2. Cut the following fabric width strips from mottled flannel fabrics: three 3½" red (A); two 8" strips orange (B); two 10" strips yellow (C); two 12" strips green (D); two 14" strips medium blue (E); two 16" strips dark blue (F); and two 18" strips light purple (G).

Step 3. Cut 30 A pieces from red strips.

Step 4. Fold the remaining colored strips in half along length with right sides out to make long double-layer strips. Lay the B template on a folded orange strip with fold edge of template on fold of fabric as shown in Figure 1; cut 30 B pieces.

Figure 1
Lay B template on a
folded orange strip.

Step 5. Repeat Step 4 with pieces C–G referring to template for color, cutting 30 of each piece.

Step 6. Cut 10 strips light blue mottled 12½" by fabric width; subcut into 12½" square segments. You will need 30 squares for background.

Step 7. To piece one block, lay one piece each A–G on a background block in alphabetical order with edges touching as shown in Figure 2. ***Note: Keep the top edge of the light purple strip ¼" below the edge of the block to prevent catching it in the block seams.***

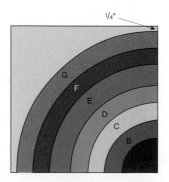

Figure 2
Lay 1 piece each A–G on a
background block in alphabetical
order with edges touching.

Step 8. Remove the A piece and apply a very light beaded line of liquid fusible web about ⅝"–¾" from the curved edge; return the piece to the background square.

Step 9. Apply the liquid fusible web down the center of each of the colored strips one at a time by folding the strips in half while still on the background square as shown in Figure 3. Fold the strip back and repeat on the second half. Continue until the liquid fusible web has been applied to all the strips. Repeat for all blocks.

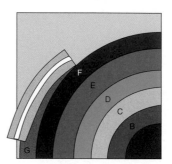

Figure 3
Fold the strips in half while still
on the background square;
apply liquid fusible web on the
center of the folded strip.

Step 10. Referring to the liquid fusible web instructions, fuse strips to blocks.

Step 11. Using rainbow variegated quilting and craft thread, stitch ½" from the curved edge of each A piece and ½" from both curved edges of the B–G pieces referring to Figure 4.

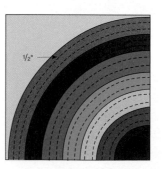

Figure 4
Stitch ½" from the curved
edges of each piece.

Step 12. Clip into each piece almost to the sewing lines as shown in Figure 5; clips should be ¼"–½" apart. ***Note: The closer the clips are together, the more the strips will fringe when washed.***

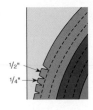

Figure 5
Clip into each piece almost to the sewing lines; clips should be 1/4"–1/2" apart.

Step 13. Arrange the blocks in six rows of five blocks each, referring to the Placement Diagram for positioning of blocks in rows to create the diagonal design. Join blocks in rows; press seams in one direction. Join rows; press seams in one direction.

Step 14. Cut and piece four 6½" x 72½" strips red mottled flannel. Sew a strip to opposite long sides and remaining strips to the top and bottom; press seams toward strips.

Finishing the Quilt

Step 1. Sandwich batting between the completed top and prepared backing piece; pin or baste layers together to hold flat for quilting.

Step 2. Quilt as desired by hand or machine. *Note: The quilt shown was machine-quilted in the ditch of block and border seams using clear nylon monofilament in the top of the machine and all-purpose thread in the bobbin.*

Step 3. When quilting is complete, trim batting and backing even with quilted top; remove pins or basting.

Step 4. Cut eight 2½" by fabric width strips red mottled flannel. Join strips on short ends to make one long strip for binding.

Step 5. Fold the binding strip in half along length with wrong sides together; press.

Step 6. Bind edges to finish.

Step 7. Wash and dry the quilt to create rag edges on strips. Be sure to clean the dryer's lint filter every five minutes. When the lint filter stops being full every five minutes, clean it every 10 minutes until the quilt is dry. *Note: A commercial dryer is another choice for successful drying.* ❖

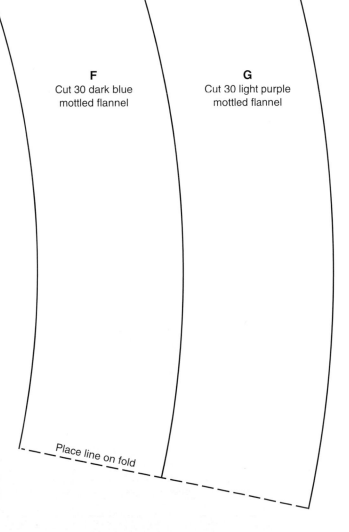

F
Cut 30 dark blue
mottled flannel

G
Cut 30 light purple
mottled flannel

Place line on fold

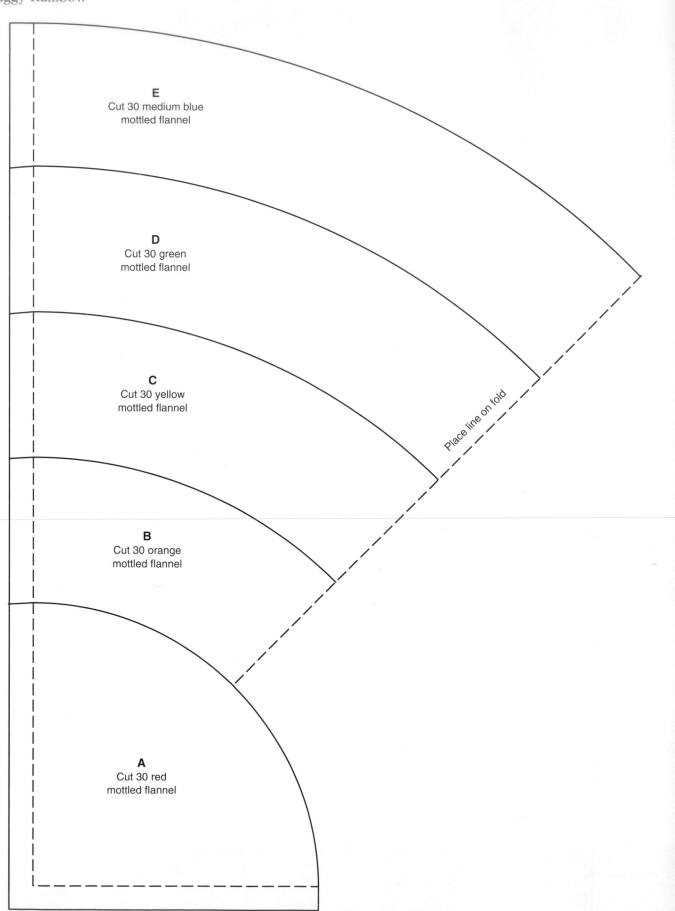

E

Cut 30 medium blue
mottled flannel

D

Cut 30 green
mottled flannel

C

Cut 30 yellow
mottled flannel

B

Cut 30 orange
mottled flannel

A

Cut 30 red
mottled flannel

Place line on fold

Bunny Hugs

By Julie Weaver

Pastel plaids and checks make the perfect background for this appliquéd bunny.

Fusible Machine Appliqué

The pieced background was sprayed with Sulky KK 2000 Temporary Spray Adhesive to hold the heart in place while machine blanket-stitches were completed. Steam-A-Seam 2 fusible transfer web was used to apply the bunny to the center heart appliqué following the manufacturer's instructions. Fabric patches were layered with the aid of The Appliqué Pressing Sheet, which allows one to arrange and rearrange pieces before fusing in place, if necessary.

Project Specifications

Skill Level: Intermediate
Quilt Size: 26" x 32"

Materials

- 4" x 6" rectangle cream homespun
- Assorted plaid scraps for bunny appliqué
- Assorted plaid scraps for pieced background ranging from 13½" x 9½" to 4½" x 2½"
- ⅜ yard light plaid for second border
- ½ yard blue plaid for first border and binding
- ¾ yard tan stripe for heart
- Batting 32" x 38"
- Backing 32" x 38"
- All-purpose thread to match fabrics
- Cream machine-quilting thread
- Pastel variegated machine-quilting thread
- No. 8 light blue pearl cotton

- ½ yard Steam-A-Seam 2 fusible transfer web
- Sulky KK 2000 Temporary Spray Adhesive
- Pink and black permanent fabric markers
- The Appliqué Pressing Sheet
- Water-soluble blue marking pen
- Basic sewing tools and supplies

Piecing the Background with Borders

Step 1. Referring to Figure 1, cut squares and rectangles in the sizes given from assorted plaids for background.

Step 2. Join the pieces in units, again referring to Figure 1; press seams toward larger unpieced

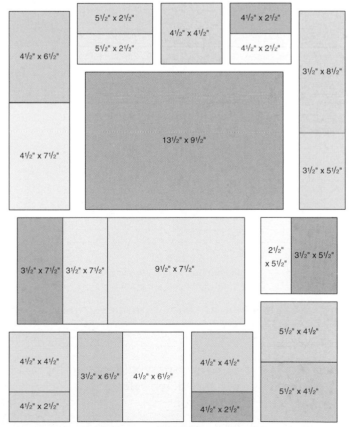

Figure 1
Cut fabric pieces from assorted plaid scraps in the sizes indicated. Join the pieces to create pieced units; join units to complete the pieced background.

units. Join the pieced units to create the pieced background; press.

Step 3. Cut two strips each 1½" x 22½" and 1½" x 26½" blue plaid; sew the longer strips to opposite sides and shorter strips to the top and bottom of the pieced center. Press seams toward strips.

Step 4. Cut two strips each 2½" x 26½" and 2½" x 28½" light plaid; sew the longer strips to opposite sides and shorter strips to the top and bottom of the pieced center; press seams toward strips.

Step 5. Fold the pieced top and crease to mark the center.

Applying Appliqué

Step 1. Create the heart pattern referring to Figure 2 to enlarge design.

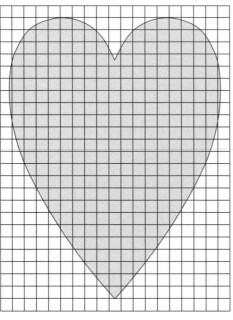

Figure 2
Make the heart template using
this graph. Each square equals 1".

Step 2. Cut one heart shape from tan stripe using the enlarged pattern. Mark the center of the heart pattern.

Step 3. Apply temporary spray adhesive to the wrong side of the heart shape referring to manufacturer's instructions.

Step 4. Center the heart shape on the pieced background matching the center of the heart with the center of the background.

Step 5. Using No. 8 light blue pearl cotton and a hand or machine blanket-stitch, stitch heart shape in place.

Step 6. Prepare templates for each appliqué shape using patterns given. Apply fusible transfer web to the wrong side of scrap fabrics chosen for bunny parts referring to manufacturer's instructions.

Step 7. Trace shapes onto the paper side of the fused scraps; cut out shapes on traced lines. Remove paper backing.

Step 8. Transfer facial features to the bunny head piece using the water-soluble blue marking pen.

Step 9. Layer shapes in numerical order on the pressing sheet referring to overlap lines on pattern pieces and Figure 3 for positioning.

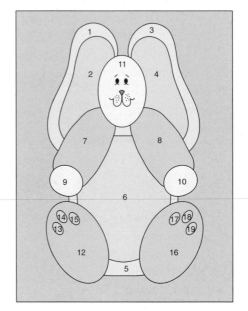

Figure 3
Layer shapes in numerical order on
the pressing sheet referring to
overlap lines on pattern pieces.

Step 10. When satisfied with placement, press appliqué shapes in place to secure. Remove the entire design from the pressing sheet and center on the heart shape. Press in place to secure.

Step 11. Appliqué each shape in place as in Step 5.

Step 12. Draw on the eyes and mouth shapes using the black permanent fabric marker; draw on the nose and whisker dots with the pink permanent fabric marker.

Step 13. Referring to Figure 4 and the Placement Diagram, draw lines from the bunny motif to the

edge of the heart motif to resemble crazy quilting sections and top hair, referring to the pattern and using the water-soluble blue marking pen.

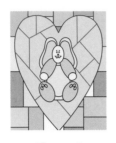

Figure 4
Draw lines from the bunny motif to the edge of the heart motif to resemble crazy quilting sections.

Step 14. Chain-stitch along marked lines using No. 8 light blue pearl cotton.

Step 15. Spray water on areas where the marks are visible to remove.

Finishing the Quilt

Step 1. Sandwich batting between the completed top and prepared backing piece; pin or baste layers together to hold flat for quilting.

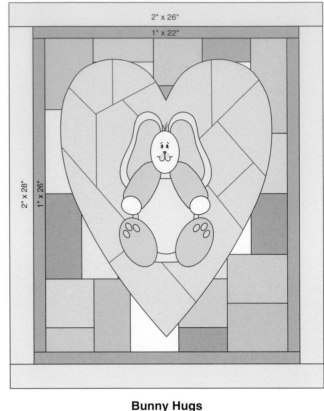

Bunny Hugs
Placement Diagram
26" x 32"

Step 2. Quilt as desired by hand or machine. *Note: The sample shown was machine-quilted in a meandering design in the background around the heart shape and in the outside border strips using pastel variegated machine-quilting thread. Outline quilting was done on each side of the chain stitches and around appliquéd motifs using cream machine-quilting thread.*

Step 3. When quilting is complete, trim batting and backing even with quilted top; remove pins or basting.

Step 4. Cut four 2¼" by fabric width strips blue plaid. Join strips on short ends to make one long strip for binding.

Step 5. Fold the binding strip in half along length with wrong sides together; press.

Step 6. Bind edges to finish. ❖

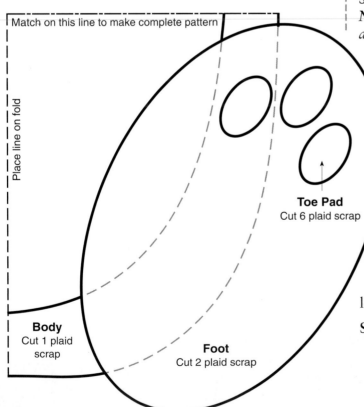

Match on this line to make complete pattern

Place line on fold

Toe Pad
Cut 6 plaid scrap

Body
Cut 1 plaid scrap

Foot
Cut 2 plaid scrap

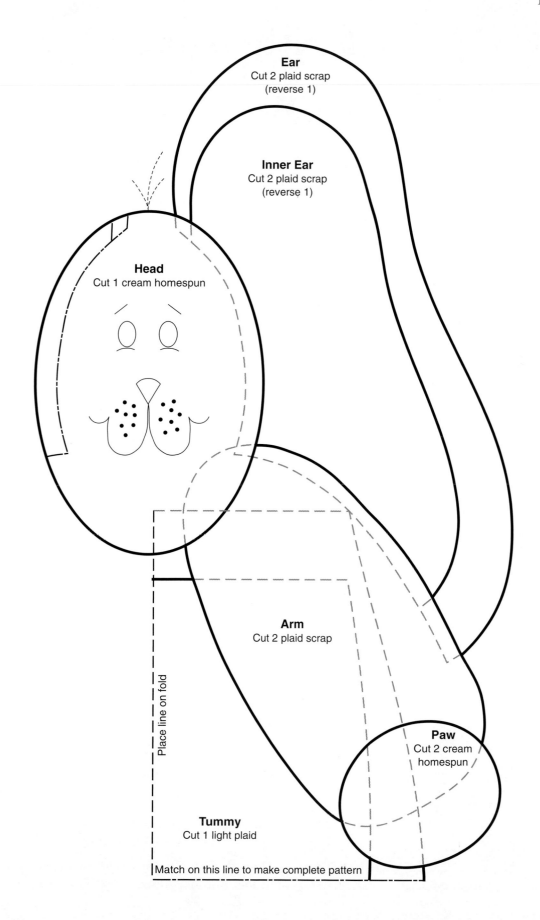

Ear
Cut 2 plaid scrap
(reverse 1)

Inner Ear
Cut 2 plaid scrap
(reverse 1)

Head
Cut 1 cream homespun

Arm
Cut 2 plaid scrap

Place line on fold

Paw
Cut 2 cream
homespun

Tummy
Cut 1 light plaid

Match on this line to make complete pattern

Lollipop Flowers

By Sue Harvey

Soft chenille flower heads make this a cuddly toddler-size quilt.

Chenille By The Inch

Chenille By The Inch can be used to create fuzzy flowers. Premade bias strips are stitched in place, dampened and brushed to create fluffy chenille-look rings.

Project Note

Fabric stabilizer is used behind each block to machine-appliqué the curved pieces, stems and leaves and to stitch the chenille strips in place. I prefer to use a solid piece of stabilizer behind the block rather than two or more pieces. To do this, twelve 12" x 12" squares of stabilizer, or 4 yards,

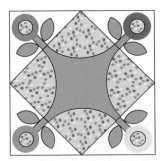

Lollipop Flowers
12" x 12" Block

are needed with approximately 10" leftover from the stabilizer width. This can be used for other projects. To use several smaller pieces of stabilizer behind each block, purchase only 2½ yards.

Project Specifications

Skill Level: Intermediate
Quilt Size: 48" x 60" (including scallops)
Block Size: 12" x 12"
Number of Blocks: 12

Materials

- 2¼ yards floral print
- 1¼ yards each white print and green tone-on-tone
- Batting 54" x 66"
- Backing 54" x 66"
- White all-purpose thread
- White machine-quilting thread
- Light green Sulky rayon thread
- 1½ yards Wonder-Under fusible transfer web
- 4 yards Stitch-n-Tear fabric stabilizer
- 1 package each Blue Moon, Banana, Grape Soda and Raspberry Chenille By The Inch
- Chenille Brush
- Chenille Cutting Guide
- Spray bottle
- 6" x 6" square lightweight plastic
- Basic sewing tools and supplies

Making A-B Units

Step 1. Cut five strips 4¼" by fabric width floral print; subcut into 48 squares 4¼" x 4¼" for A.

Step 2. Cut three strips 9" by fabric width green tone-on-tone; subcut into 12 squares 9" x 9" for B.

Step 3. Prepare template for D; trace 48 D pieces on the paper side of the fusible transfer web. Cut out each piece.

Step 4. Place a D piece on the wrong side of an A square, aligning edges of D with edges of A as shown in Figure 1; fuse in place.

Figure 1
Place D on the
wrong side of A.

Figure 2
Trim A even with
curved edge of D.

Step 5. Trim A square even with outer curved edge of D as shown in Figure 2; repeat with all A squares. Remove paper backing from D pieces.

Step 6. Place an A piece on one corner of B, aligning corner and edges of A with corner and edges of B as shown in Figure 3; fuse in place.

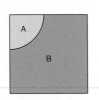

Figure 3
Place A on 1 corner of B.

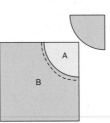

Figure 4
Trim away B under A.

Step 7. Trim away the unfused green tone-on-tone section under the A piece as shown in Figure 4. Repeat on all corners of each B square to complete 12 A-B units.

Making C Units

Step 1. Cut four strips 6⅞" by fabric width white print; subcut into 6⅞" square segments. Cut each square in half on one diagonal to make 48 C triangles.

Step 2. Cut one strip 3½" by fabric width floral print and three strips 3¼" x 18" fusible transfer web. Apply fusible transfer web to the wrong side of the floral print strip.

Step 3. Cut one strip 9" by fabric width green tone-on-tone and three strips 8½" x 18" fusible transfer web. Apply fusible transfer web to the wrong side of the green tone-on-tone strip.

Step 4. Cut one strip 2" by fabric width from the fused green tone-on-tone strip; subcut into ½" segments for stems. You will need 48 stems; remove paper backing.

Step 5. Prepare templates for the flower center and leaf pieces. Trace 48 flower center pieces on the paper side of the fused floral print strip; cut out each piece and remove paper backing.

Step 6. Trace 96 leaf pieces on the paper side of the fused green tone-on-tone strip; cut out each piece and remove paper backing.

Step 7. Arrange one stem, one flower center and two leaf pieces on each C triangle, centering the stem piece on the long side of the triangle as shown in Figure 5; fuse pieces in place.

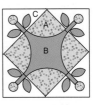

Figure 5
Arrange the flower pieces on C.

Completing the Blocks

Step 1. Center and sew a C unit to each side of an A-B unit as shown in Figure 6; press seams toward C. Repeat for 12 A-B-C units.

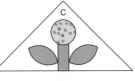

Figure 6
Sew a C unit to each side of A-B.

Step 2. Cut 12 squares 12" x 12" fabric stabilizer; pin one square on the wrong side of each unit.

Step 3. Using light green rayon thread in the top of the machine and white all-purpose thread in the bobbin, machine buttonhole-stitch along the curved A edges and the stem and leaf pieces. Do not stitch around the flower center pieces.

Step 4. Prepare 70" of each color of chenille strips, referring to manufacturer's instructions.

Step 5. Stitch a purple chenille strip around the edge of one flower center piece on an A-B-C unit, overlapping ends of strip about ¼"; trim strip.

Step 6. Repeat with remaining colors on each of the remaining flower center pieces to complete one block as shown in Figure 7. Repeat with all A-B-C units to make 12 blocks, placing the chenille strips in the same color order on each block. Do not brush the chenille strips.

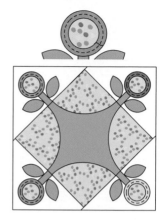

Figure 7
Stitch chenille strips around each flower center piece to complete 1 block.

Completing the Top

Step 1. Join three blocks to make a row as shown in Figure 8; repeat for four rows. Press seams in two rows in one direction and in the remaining rows in the opposite direction.

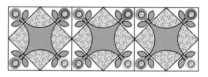

Figure 8
Join 3 blocks to make a row.

Step 2. Join rows to complete the pieced center, alternating pressed rows to offset seams; press seams in one direction.

Step 3. Cut (and piece) two strips each 1½" x 38½" and 1½" x 48½" white print. Sew the longer strips to opposite long sides and shorter strips to the top and bottom of the pieced center; press seams toward strips.

Step 4. Cut and piece two strips each 3½" x 44½" and 3½" x 50½" floral print. Sew the longer strips to opposite long sides and shorter strips to the top and bottom of the pieced center; press seams toward strips.

Step 5. In the center of the light-weight plastic square, mark a circle that is ⅛" inch larger in circumference than the flower center piece; cut out circle.

Step 6. Place opening of the plastic square over one flower circle with edges of plastic under chenille strip as shown in Figure 9; vigorously brush chenille strip. Spray lightly with water; brush until strip is fluffy. **Note:** *The plastic square protects the buttonhole stitches and surrounding fabric from the stiff bristles of the brush and prevents fuzz from coating the white print fabric around each flower.*

Figure 9
Place plastic square opening over 1 flower circle.

Finishing the Quilt

Step 1. Sandwich the batting between the completed top and prepared backing piece; pin or baste to hold layers together.

Step 2. Quilt as desired by hand or machine, stopping stitches 1" from the outer edge of the floral print border. **Note:** *The sample shown was professionally machine-quilted using white machine-quilting thread.*

Step 3. Trim batting and backing even with quilted top; remove pins or basting. Fold the backing edge down away from the quilt edge; pin or baste in place.

Step 4. Cut seven strips 4½" by fabric width floral print. Fold each strip in half across width with right sides together; subcut into 2½" segments. You will need 50 segment pairs.

Step 5. Prepare a template for E. Trace E on one side of each segment pair, aligning the straight edge of E with a long edge of the segment as shown in Figure 10.

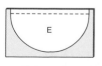

Figure 10
Trace E on 1 side of each segment pair.

Step 6. Stitch each pair on the marked line; trim seam allowance, turn right side out and press flat to complete scallop shapes.

Step 7. Pin 14 scallop shapes along one long side of the quilted top, beginning and ending ¼ " from corners as shown in Figure 11; stitch in place through top and batting layers only. Repeat on the opposite side. Arrange and stitch 11 scallop shapes each on the top and bottom edges.

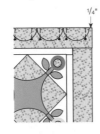

Figure 11
Pin scallop shapes
along 1 side.

Step 8. Trim batting close to stitching line. Fold the scallop pieces out and the seam allowance to the back of the quilt; press lightly.

Step 9. Release the backing fabric; turn raw edge in ¼ " and press. Pin in place around scallop edge. Hand- or machine-stitch in place.

Step 10. Hand- or machine-quilt ½ " from edge of floral print border to finish. ❖

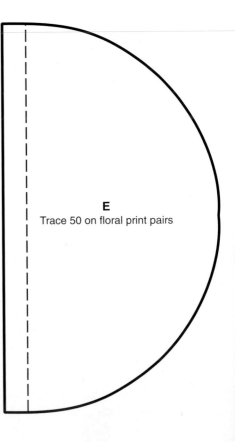

Lollipop Flowers
Placement Diagram
48" x 60"
(including scallops)

D
Trace
48
fusible
web

E
Trace 50 on floral print pairs

Flower Center
Cut 48 floral print

Leaf
Cut 96 green
tone-on-tone

Baby's Stars Quilt

By Connie Kauffman

Appliqué star shapes to a background pieced from varying-width fabric strips.

Spray Adhesive Appliqué

Eliminate fusible transfer web when using Sulky KK 2000 Temporary Spray Adhesive to adhere motifs in place for machine appliqué.

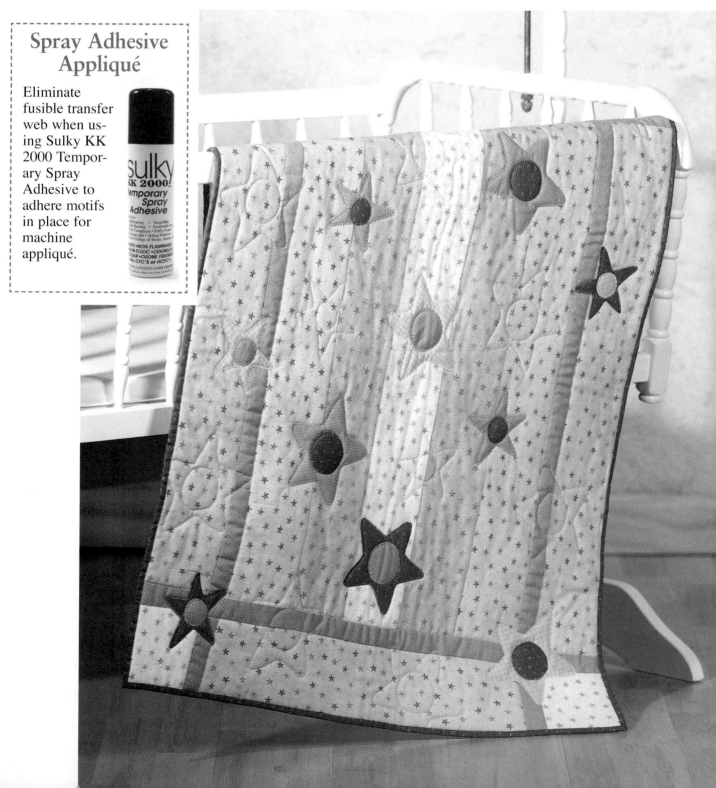

Project Specifications

Skill Level: Beginner

Quilt Size: 26½" x 34"

Materials

- ¼ yard yellow tone-on-tone
- ¼ yard each white, yellow and blue star prints
- ⅜ yard pink dot
- ⅜ yard green star print
- ½ yard purple tone-on-tone
- Batting 33" x 40"
- Backing 33" x 40"
- Neutral color all-purpose thread
- Sulky pink, lavender and yellow rayon thread
- Sulky KK 2000 Temporary Spray Adhesive
- Basic sewing tools and supplies and water-erasable marker or pencil

Making Pieced Background

Step 1. Cut one strip white star print and two strips each green, blue and yellow star prints 4" x 25½".

Step 2. Cut two strips pink dot 1½" x 25½".

Step 3. Join the strips referring to Figure 1 for color placement; press seams of center panel in one direction and the outside border strips toward the pink dot strips.

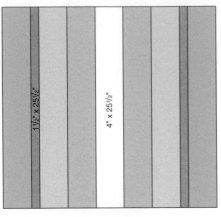

1½" x 25½"

4" x 25½"

Figure 1
Join the strips in the order shown.

Step 4. Cut four squares white star print 4" x 4", two strips 1½" x 4" pink dot and two strips green star print 4" x 18". Join squares and strips to make top and bottom strips as shown in Figure 2; press seams toward the pink dot strips.

1½" x 4"

4"
x 4"

4" x 18"

Figure 2
Join the squares and strips as shown.

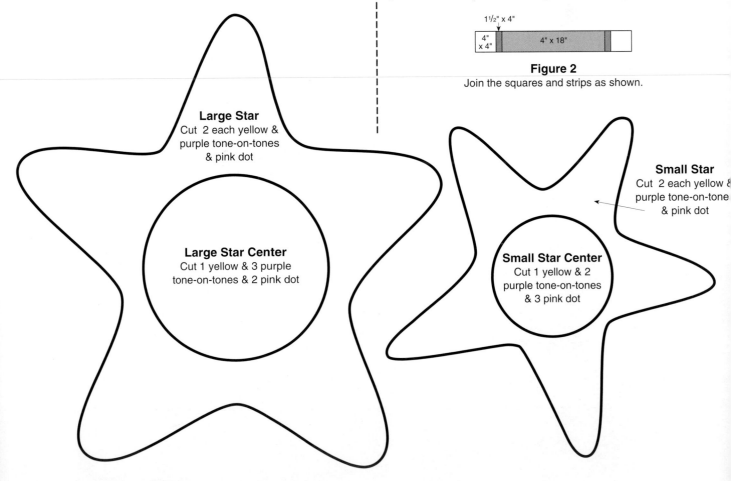

Large Star
Cut 2 each yellow &
purple tone-on-tones
& pink dot

Large Star Center
Cut 1 yellow & 3 purple
tone-on-tones & 2 pink dot

Small Star
Cut 2 each yellow &
purple tone-on-tone
& pink dot

Small Star Center
Cut 1 yellow & 2
purple tone-on-tones
& 3 pink dot

Step 5. Cut two strips 1½" x 27" pink dot; sew a strip to the top and bottom border strips referring to Figure 3; press seams toward pink dot strips. Sew a strip to the top and bottom of the previously pieced section to complete the pieced background referring to Figure 4.

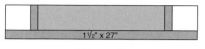

Figure 3
Sew a 1½" x 27" pink dot
strip to the pieced strip.

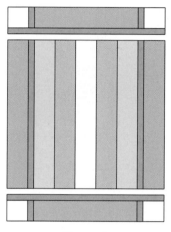

Figure 4
Join strips and pieced unit to
complete the pieced background.

Completing Star Appliqué

Step 1. Prepare templates for star shapes using patterns given; cut as directed on each piece.

Step 2. Open a paper bag and lay flat on a flat surface; very lightly spray the surface of the bag with spray adhesive.

Step 3. Lay each appliqué shape right side down on the sprayed bag; referring to manufacturer's instructions, apply spray adhesive to each piece.

Step 4. Arrange the star motifs on the pieced background referring to the Placement Diagram for positioning of colors.

Finishing the Quilt

Step 1. Using the star templates, mark large and small star shapes randomly over the background area using a water-erasable marker or pencil.

Step 2. Sandwich batting between the completed top and prepared backing piece; pin or baste layers together to hold flat for quilting.

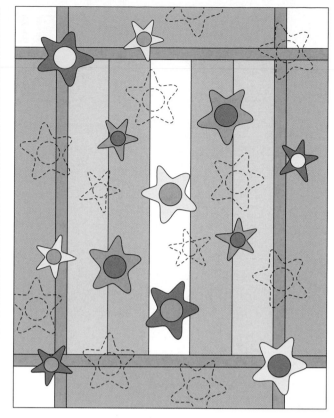

Baby's Stars Quilt
Placement Diagram
26½" x 34"

Step 3. Quilt as desired by hand or machine. *Note: The sample shown was machine-quilted on the star shapes and in the ditch of seams of the pink dot border pieces using pink rayon thread.*

Step 4. When quilting is complete, trim batting and backing even with quilted top; remove pins or basting.

Step 5. Cut four 2¼" by fabric width strips purple tone-on-tone. Join strips on short ends to make one long strip for binding.

Step 6. Fold the binding strip in half along length with wrong sides together; press.

Step 7. Bind edges to finish.

Step 8. Using appliqué thread to match appliqué pieces in the top of the machine and all-purpose thread in the bobbin and a narrow machine blanket or buttonhole stitch, stitch around each star shape and center to secure through all layers to finish. ❖

Twinkle, Twinkle Little Star

By Sue Kruger

If you love to paint and quilt, combine your hobbies in this child's quilt based on a familiar song.

Paint-and-Fuse Appliqué

Fabrics may be highlighted and features added to shapes using fabric paints and then appliquéd to a background using fusible transfer web. The shapes may then be straight-stitched in place to secure.

Man in the Moon
6½" x 9¾" Block

Planets
6½" x 9¾" Block

Stars
6½" x 9¾" Block

Sun
6½" x 9¾" Block

Twinkle Star
6½" x 9¾" Block

Project Specifications
Skill Level: Intermediate
Quilt Size: 37½" x 47¼"
Block Size: 6½" x 9¾"
Number of Blocks: 9

Materials
- Scraps for small planets
- Scraps light green and red mottleds for moon and hearts
- 6" x 6" scrap blue/green solid for large planet
- ⅛ yard dark blue mottled
- ¼ yard white-on-white print
- ¼ yard 3 different yellow mottleds or solids for stars, moon and sun—1 should be bright yellow
- ½ yard deep blue mottled
- ⅔ yard light blue mottled
- 1¼ yards medium blue mottled
- Batting 43" x 53"
- Backing 43" x 53"
- Neutral color all-purpose thread
- Clear nylon monofilament
- Black Sakura Identi-Pen fine-point permanent marker
- Teflon sheet
- 1½ yards lightweight fusible transfer web
- Flesh, black, white, navy blue and burnt sienna DecoArt Americana acrylic paints
- DecoArt Americana fabric painting medium
- No. 10 flat, No. 6 flat and No. 1 liner brushes
- Basic sewing tools and supplies

Basic Painting Technique

Step 1. Set up work space with a cup of clean water, paint palette and good paper towels. After using brushes, rinse well in water container. Pour out small amounts of paints and add fabric medium.

Step 2. All shading is done using flat brushes that fit the area. Shading is putting paint on one side of the brush and small amount of fabric medium on the other side. Blend together by working your brush back and forth on your paint palette.

Step 3. When finished blending, one side should shade to nothing. Practice to get the best results.

Preparing Appliquéd & Painted Motifs

Step 1. Trace appliqué motifs onto the paper side of the fusible transfer web referring to patterns for number to cut. Trace all pieces to be cut from the same fabrics together in a group. Cut out shapes in groups, leaving a margin around each group. *Note: Shapes are given in reverse for fusible machine appliqué.*

Step 2. Fuse the traced shapes onto the wrong side of the fabrics as directed on each piece for color.

Step 3. Cut out shapes on traced lines; remove paper backing.

Step 4. Fuse several shapes to the Teflon sheet to prepare for painting. *Note: Fuse moon, hat and small star together as one shape.*

Step 5. Paint stars and twinkle star with a wash of burnt sienna. Add paint to only one side of the stars. Do this with all small- and medium-size stars. When completely dry, add stitch lines with black fine-point permanent marker.

Step 6. Add white eyes in the shape of small ovals on the twinkle star shape. Dry and add a black dot to one corner of each eye. When black is dry, add a highlight of white.

Step 7. Cheeks and nose are painted with a wash of flesh, keeping the colors very light. Add a dot of white highlight to the top of the cheek and nose.

Step 8. After the paint is dry, use the black fine-point permanent marker to add mouth, nose, outline eyes, eyebrows and freckles. Shade the bow tie with navy blue and highlight with white.

Step 9. Shade one side of the large planet with navy blue. Dry-brush some color into the interior with both the navy and white. If necessary, the smaller planets can be dry-brushed with white or burnt sienna to add color.

Step 10. Shade the bottom half of the outside edge of the sun with flesh. Add a white highlight to the top edge. Shade the inside circle with flesh. Using a wash of flesh, shade the eyes, nose and cheek areas. Add detail lines with black fine-point permanent marker after paint is dry.

Step 11. Add details to moon using the fine-point permanent marker. Use a wash of burnt sienna around the outside edges; paint cheeks and lips with a wash of flesh. Paint white oval for eye and add black dot. Add white highlight to top of cheek and eye.

Step 12. After background is prepared, peel shapes off the Teflon sheet.

Completing the Quilt Top

Step 1. Cut nine 7" x 10¼" rectangles light blue mottled for background.

Step 2. Cut six 2½" x 10½" strips medium blue mottled (A) and six 2½" x 7" strips deep blue mottled (B).

Step 3. Cut two 2⅞" x 2⅞" squares each medium blue (C) and dark blue (D) mottleds. Cut each square in half on one diagonal to make C and D triangles.

Step 4. Sew a C triangle to a D triangle to make a C-D unit as shown in Figure 1; repeat for four units.

Figure 1
Sew a C triangle to a D
triangle to make a C-D unit.

Step 5. Fuse painted shapes to background squares referring to the block drawings for positioning of pieces. Use the fine-point permanent marker to make lines connecting heart shapes and one star to moon referring to the block drawing.

Step 6. Arrange the fused blocks with the plain rectangles to make three rows of three blocks each referring to the Placement Diagram for positioning.

Step 7. Join three blocks with A to make a block

row as shown in Figure 2; repeat for three rows. Press seams toward A.

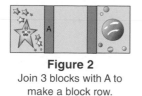

Figure 2
Join 3 blocks with A to
make a block row.

Step 8. Join two C-D units with three B pieces to make a sashing row referring to Figure 3; repeat for two sashing rows. Press seams away from B.

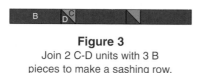

Figure 3
Join 2 C-D units with 3 B
pieces to make a sashing row.

Step 9. Join the block rows with the sashing rows to complete the pieced center; press seams toward sashing rows.

Step 10. Cut one strip each 3" x 24" and 3" x 36¼" white-on-white print. Sew the shorter strip to the top and longer strip to the right side edge of the pieced center; press seams toward strips.

Step 11. Arrange letters to spell the words Twinkle Twinkle across the top and Little Star down the side on the strips; fuse in place. Arrange and fuse two small stars between words on top strip and above, between and below words on side strip referring to the Placement Diagram for positioning.

Step 12. Cut two strips each 1¾" x 29" and 1¾" x 36¼" deep blue mottled. Sew the longer strips to opposite long sides and shorter strips to the top and bottom of the completed center; press seams toward strips.

Step 13. Cut two strips each 5" x 38" and 5" x 38¾" medium blue mottled. Sew the longer strips to opposite sides and shorter strips to the top and bottom of the completed center; press seams toward strips.

Finishing the Quilt

Step 1. Sandwich batting between the completed top and prepared backing piece; pin or baste

Twinkle, Twinkle Little Star
Placement Diagram
37½" x 47¼"

layers together to hold flat for quilting.

Step 2. Quilt as desired by hand or machine. *Note: The quilt shown was machine-quilted in a meandering and star design in block backgrounds, with straight stitches on edges of fused shapes, in a swirling design in A and B pieces and in a meandering and star design on border strips using clear nylon monofilament in the top of the machine and all-purpose thread in the bobbin.*

Step 3. When quilting is complete, trim batting and backing even with quilted top; remove pins or basting.

Step 4. Cut five 2¼" by fabric width strips medium blue mottled. Join strips on short ends to make one long strip for binding.

Step 5. Fold the binding strip in half along length with wrong sides together; press.

Step 6. Bind edges to finish. ❖

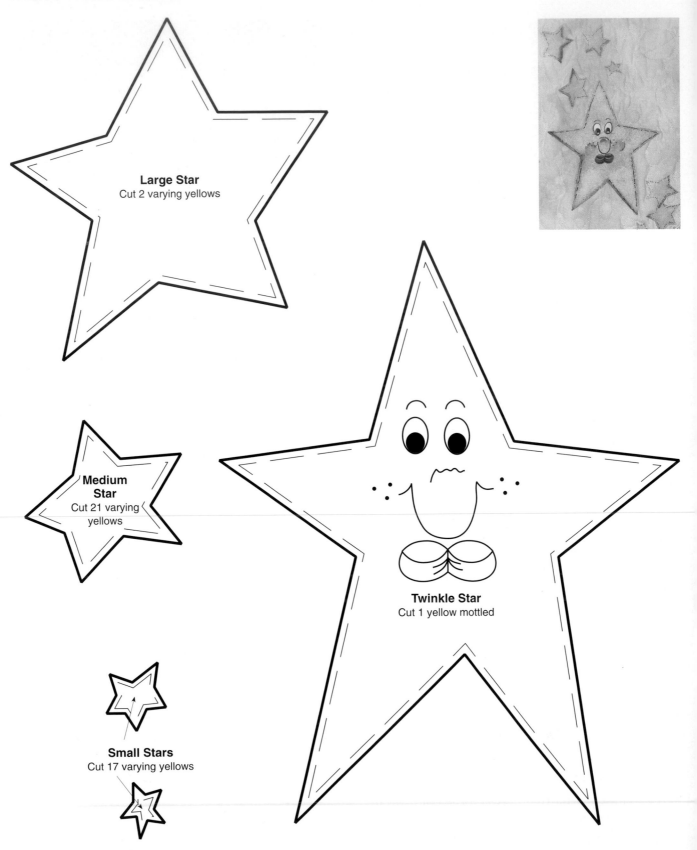

Large Star
Cut 2 varying yellows

Medium Star
Cut 21 varying yellows

Small Stars
Cut 17 varying yellows

Twinkle Star
Cut 1 yellow mottled

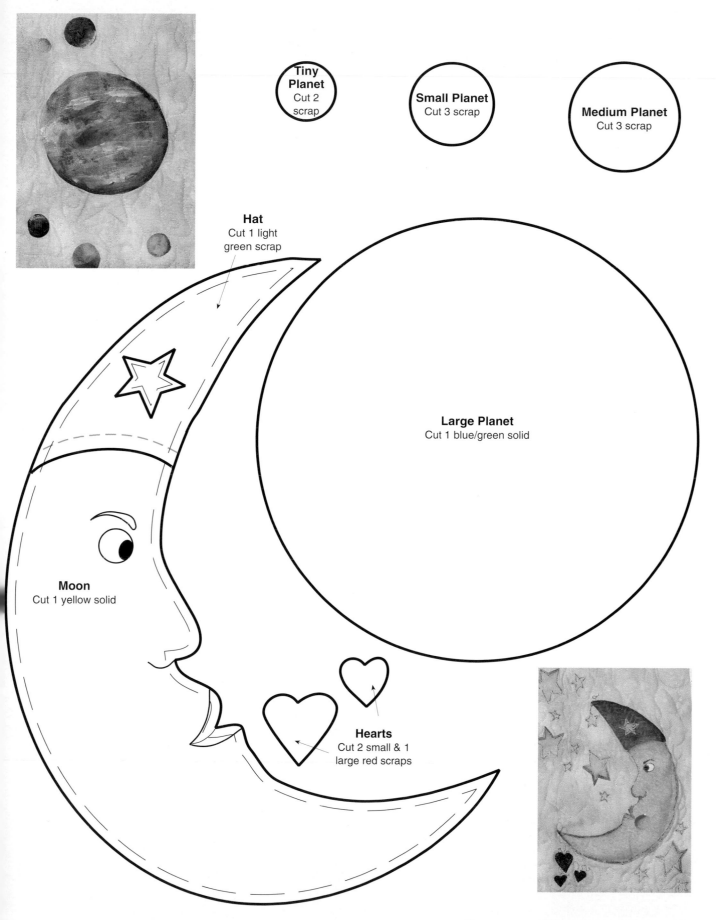

Tiny Planet
Cut 2 scrap

Small Planet
Cut 3 scrap

Medium Planet
Cut 3 scrap

Hat
Cut 1 light green scrap

Large Planet
Cut 1 blue/green solid

Moon
Cut 1 yellow solid

Hearts
Cut 2 small & 1 large red scraps

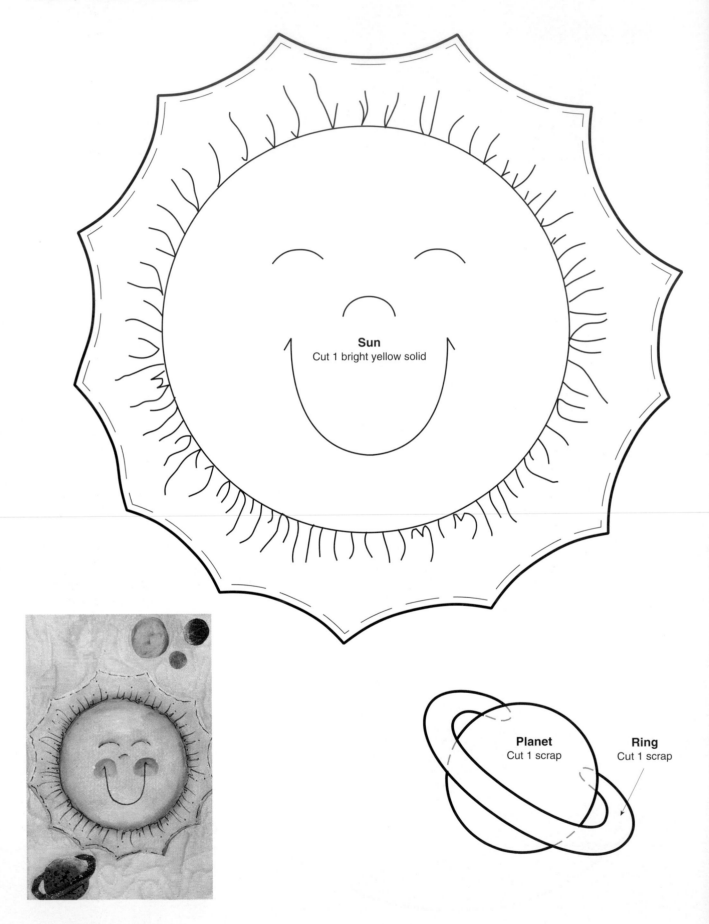

Sun
Cut 1 bright yellow solid

Planet
Cut 1 scrap

Ring
Cut 1 scrap

Letters
Cut 1 each A, R & S, 2 each K, N & W, 3 each E & I, 4 L & 5 T dark blue mottled

Cartwheel Clowns

By Judith Sandstrom

Bright-colored clowns are tumbling all over this quilt top.

Fusible Machine Appliqué

Trace patterns on the paper side of the fusible transfer web, fuse to fabrics, cut out, remove paper, position and fuse in place before stitching.

Cartwheel Clown
9" x 9" Block

Project Specifications

Skill Level: Intermediate
Quilt Size: 43½" x 54"
Block Size: 9" x 9"
Number of Blocks: 20

Materials

- ⅙ yard each black and peach solids
- ⅜ yard each 12 bright prints
- ½ yard blue print for sashing squares and binding
- 1½ yards white-on-white print
- Thin batting 49" x 60"
- Backing 49" x 60"
- All-purpose thread to match bright prints and black and peach
- White machine-quilting thread
- 2¼ yards Wonder-Under fusible transfer web
- 1½ yards ½"-wide white lace
- Black, blue, red and brown fine-point Pigma pens or fabric pens
- Basic sewing tools and supplies

Making Clown Blocks

Step 1. Prewash and iron all fabrics before cutting.

Cartwheel Clowns
Placement Diagram
43½" x 54"

Step 2. Cut two 2" by fabric width strips from each of the 12 bright prints; set aside.

Step 3. Prepare templates for clown shapes using the full-size pattern given; transfer details to templates. Referring to patterns for number to cut, trace all face, hand and shoe shapes in one area on the paper side of the fusible transfer web, reversing half of the shoe pieces. Cut out the entire area and fuse the traced face and hand sections to the wrong side of the peach solid and the traced shoe section to the black solid.

Step 4. Cut out shapes on traced lines; remove paper backing. Place each face piece on pattern and add eyes with blue and black Pigma pens and mouth with red Pigma pen.

Step 5. Trace clown suit and hat shapes on the paper side of the fusible transfer web as directed on patterns for number to cut. Cut out each shape, leaving a margin around each one.

Step 6. Fuse clown suit and hat shapes to the wrong side of the bright prints, making one of some fabrics and two of others. Cut hats to match each clown suit; remove paper backing.

Step 7. Cut 20 squares white-on-white print 9½" x 9½" for background. Fold and crease to mark center.

Step 8. Cut twenty 2" pieces of 1½"-wide white lace for clown collars.

Step 9. Arrange one clown motif in the center of each square in numerical order; tuck the raw edge of one piece of lace under the head piece. Fuse shapes in place with lace under head referring to manufacturer's instructions.

Step 10. Using the brown Pigma pen, draw curly hair on the sides of the face and along bottom edge of hat of each fused clown motif; press to set.

Quilt Top Construction

Step 1. Randomly stitch the 2"-wide bright print strips in groups of three with right sides together along length, using different color combinations for strips in each group; press seams open.

Step 2. Subcut each strip set into 2" segments for A as shown in Figure 1. Join two A segments on the short ends to make an A strip as shown

in Figure 2; you will need 49 A strips. Set aside remaining segments for another project.

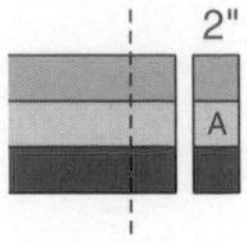

Figure 1
Subcut each strip set
into 2" segments for A.

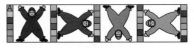

Figure 2
Join 2 A segments
on the short ends
to make an A strip.

Step 3. Arrange the blocks in five rows of four blocks each referring to the Placement Diagram for positioning of blocks. Join the blocks in rows with five A strips as shown in Figure 3; press seams away from blocks. Repeat for five rows.

Figure 3
Join the blocks in rows with 5 A strips.

Step 4. Cut two 2" by fabric width strips blue print; subcut into 2" square segments for B. You will need 30 B squares.

Step 5. Join four A strips with five B squares to make a sashing row as shown in Figure 4; repeat for six sashing rows. Press seams toward B.

B A

Figure 4
Join 4 strips with 5 B squares
to make a sashing row.

Step 6. Join the block rows with the sashing rows referring to the Placement Diagram for positioning; press seams away from blocks.

Finishing the Quilt

Step 1. Sandwich batting between the completed top and prepared backing piece; pin or baste layers together to hold flat for quilting.

Step 2. Using all-purpose thread to match fabric in the top of the machine and white-all-purpose thread in the bobbin, machine-appliqué clown pieces in place with a medium-width zig-zag stitch.

Step 3. Quilt as desired by hand or machine. *Note: The quilt shown was machine-quilted in the ditch of block seams using white machine-quilting thread.*

Step 4. When quilting is complete, trim batting and backing even with quilted top; remove pins or basting.

Step 5. Cut five 2¼" by fabric width strips blue print. Join strips on short ends to make one long strip for binding.

Step 6. Fold the binding strip in half along length with wrong sides together; press.

Step 7. Bind edges to finish. ❖

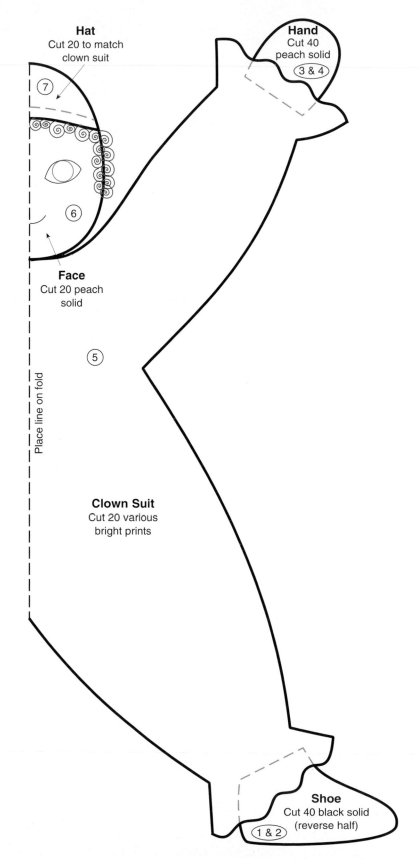

Hat
Cut 20 to match
clown suit

⑦

Hand
Cut 40
peach solid
3 & 4

⑥

Face
Cut 20 peach
solid

⑤

Place line on fold

Clown Suit
Cut 20 various
bright prints

Shoe
Cut 40 black solid
(reverse half)
1 & 2

Pastel Hearts Baby Quilt

By Connie Kauffman

Save those used dryer sheets to use in this simple appliqué method.

Dryer Sheet Appliqué

Any brand of used dryer sheet works perfectly in this method of creating a double-layer heart shape with perfect curves.

The thin dryer sheet does not add bulk to the appliqué piece and creates a soft shape.

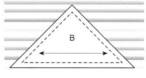

Project Specifications

Skill Level: Beginner

Quilt Size: 33" x 38"

Block Size: 5" x 5"

Number of Blocks: 30

Materials

- 1 fat quarter each blue and green tone-on-tones
- ⅜ yard pink tone-on-tone
- ½ yard yellow tone-on-tone
- 1¼ yards pastel stripe
- Fusible batting 39" x 44"
- Backing 39" x 44"
- All-purpose thread to match fabrics
- Sulky pastel variegated rayon thread
- 6 used dryer sheets
- Basic sewing tools and supplies

Instructions

Step 1. Cut two strips each 1½" x 33½" and 1½" x 38½" pink tone-on-tone; set aside for borders. Cut four 2¼" by fabric width strips yellow tone-on-tone; set aside for binding.

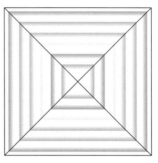

B Block
5" x 5" Block

Heart
5" x 5" Block

Step 2. Cut the following 5½" x 5½" squares from the tone-on-tone fabrics: four each pink, blue and yellow and three green for A.

Step 3. Prepare template for B using pattern given; cut as directed on the piece with stripes aligning with the diagonal of the triangle as shown in Figure 1.

Figure 1
Align stripe of fabric with long diagonal edge of B as shown.

Figure 2
Join 2 B pieces, matching stripes.

Step 4. Join two B pieces, matching stripes as shown in Figure 2; press seam in one direction. Repeat for all B pieces.

Step 5. Join two B units to complete one B block as shown in Figure 3; repeat for 15 blocks. Press seams in one direction.

Step 6. Press the used dryer sheets flat with a warm iron. Lay a used dryer sheet

Figure 3
Join 2 B units to complete 1 B block.

over the heart pattern; trace onto the used dryer sheet. Repeat for 15 traced heart shapes.

Step 7. Lay one dryer sheet against the right side of one pastel tone-on-tone fabric; pin. Sew on the marked line on the dryer sheet as shown in Figure 4; repeat for four each pink, blue and yellow tone-on-tones and three green tone-on-tone hearts. Cut out shapes leaving ⅛" beyond stitched lines referring to Figure 5.

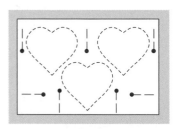

Figure 4
Sew on the marked
line on the dryer sheet.

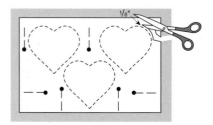

Figure 5
Cut out shapes leaving ⅛"
beyond stitched lines.

Step 8. Clip the inner point and cut off bottom point of each stitched shape as shown in Figure 6.

Figure 6
Clip the inner point and
cut off bottom point of
each stitched shape.

Figure 7
Make a ½" slit in
the dryer sheet.

Step 9. Make a ½" slit in the dryer sheet as shown in Figure 7; turn heart shapes right side out through the slit.

Step 10. Finger-press flat; press with iron.

Step 11. Center one heart shape on each A square

referring to the Placement Diagram for color placement; pin in place. Using a machine blanket or buttonhole stitch and pastel variegated rayon thread, stitch around each heart shape to complete one Heart block as shown in Figure 8.

Figure 8
Stitch around each
heart shape to
complete 1 Heart block.

Step 12. Referring to the Placement Diagram, join three B blocks with two Heart blocks to complete a row; repeat for three rows. Press seams toward Heart blocks.

Step 13. Referring to the Placement Diagram, join three Heart blocks with two B blocks to complete a row; repeat for three rows. Press seams toward Heart blocks.

Step 14. Join the rows to complete the pieced top; press seams in one direction.

Step 15. Cut two strips each 3½" x 33½" and 3½" x 38½" along length of pastel stripe.

Step 16. Sew a 1½" x 33½" pink tone-on-tone strip cut in Step 1 to a 3½" x 33½" pastel stripe strip with right sides together along length; press seams toward pastel print strip. Repeat for two strips. Repeat with the remaining strips to make side border strips.

Step 17. Sew the shorter strips to the top and bottom and longer strips to opposite long sides of the pieced center, mitering corners; press seams toward strips.

Finishing the Quilt

Step 1. Place the fusible batting on the ironing board; place the backing on top with wrong side against batting. Fuse layers together referring to manufacturer's instructions; repeat with completed top on opposite side of batting.

Step 2. Quilt as desired by hand or machine. *Note: The sample shown was machine-quilted in curv-*

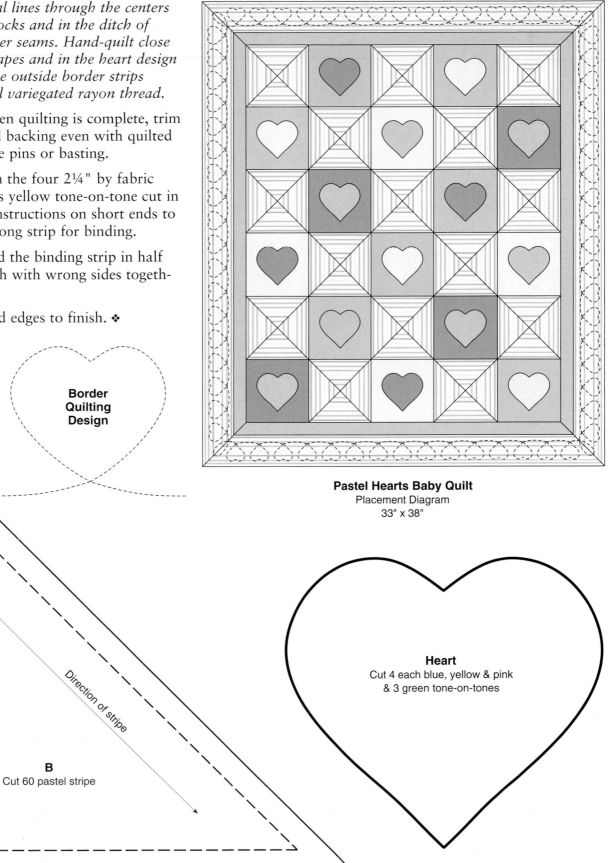

ing diagonal lines through the centers of the B blocks and in the ditch of inside border seams. Hand-quilt close to heart shapes and in the heart design given on the outside border strips using pastel variegated rayon thread.

Step 3. When quilting is complete, trim batting and backing even with quilted top; remove pins or basting.

Step 4. Join the four 2¼" by fabric width strips yellow tone-on-tone cut in Step 1 of Instructions on short ends to make one long strip for binding.

Step 5. Fold the binding strip in half along length with wrong sides together; press.

Step 6. Bind edges to finish. ❖

Border Quilting Design

Pastel Hearts Baby Quilt
Placement Diagram
33" x 38"

Heart
Cut 4 each blue, yellow & pink
& 3 green tone-on-tones

B
Cut 60 pastel stripe

Direction of stripe

Zebra Kid's Quilt

By Mary Ayres

Strange-color zebras dance in all directions across the top of this crib quilt.

Hand-Stitched Buttonhole Stitch on Fused Appliqué

Use iron-on adhesive to bond appliqué shapes to the background squares and hand-stitch in place using 3 strands of embroidery floss and a buttonhole stitch.

Project Specifications

Skill Level: Intermediate
Quilt Size: 40" x 40"
Block Size: 7" x 7"
Number of Blocks: 9

Zebra
7" x 7" Block

Materials

- 9 different 6" x 6" squares black-and-color stripe for zebras
- 1 yard magenta sub-tle stripe for background blocks and outside border strips
- 1¼ yards magenta-and-white stripe for A, B and C pieces and binding
- Batting 46" x 46"
- Backing 46" x 46"
- Black and magenta all-purpose thread
- Black 6-strand embroidery floss
- Magenta hand-quilting thread
- 2 yards black jumbo rickrack
- ¾ yard HeatnBond Lite iron-on adhesive
- Basic sewing tools and supplies

Making Zebra Blocks

Step 1. Prewash and iron all fabrics before cutting.

Step 2. Trace nine of the zebra pattern onto the paper side of the iron-on adhesive; cut out shapes leaving a margin around each one. *Note: Shape has been reversed for fusible machine appliqué.*

Step 3. Fuse one paper shape to the wrong side of each of the nine black-and-color stripe squares; cut out shapes on traced lines. Remove paper backing.

Step 4. Cut four 2¼" x 43" strips along length of the magenta-and-white stripe for binding; set aside. Cut four 4" x 33½" strips along the length

Figure 1
Pin a zebra in a corner of each of the squares with background stripes going in the same direction in each square.

of the magenta subtle stripe for border strips; set aside. Cut nine 7½" x 7½" squares magenta subtle stripe; place and pin a zebra in a corner of each of the squares with background stripes going in the same direction in each square referring to Figure 1.

Step 5. Cut nine 2½"-long (for mane)and nine 3"-long (for tail) pieces of black jumbo rickrack.

Step 6. Tuck a 3" piece of rickrack under body for tail referring to pattern for positioning; hand-stitch in place using black all-purpose thread. Repeat with a 2½" mane piece. Repeat for all blocks.

Step 7. Fuse zebra pieces in place over mane and tail pieces.

Step 8. Using 3 strands of black embroidery floss, hand-embroider a blanket stitch around edges of zebra as shown in Figure 2

Figure 2
Hand-embroider a blanket stitch around edges of zebra.

(except for foot ends that are included in block seams) to complete blocks.

Quilt Top Construction

Step 1. Prepare templates for A, B and C pieces using patterns given; cut as directed on each piece, matching marked line on A and B pieces to the center of one stripe as shown in Figure 3. *Note: It is important to match this line to the center of the same stripe for stripes to create the design at A-B intersections as shown in Figure 4.*

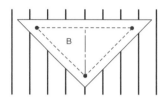

Figure 3
Match marked line on template
to the center of 1 stripe.

Figure 4
The intersection of the A-B
pieces creates an interesting
stripe design as shown.

Step 2. Arrange the appliquéd blocks on a flat surface referring to the Placement Diagram for positioning of zebras.

Step 3. Join three blocks and four A pieces to make a row as shown in Figure 5, stopping stitching at the marked dots on each A piece as shown in Figure 6; press seams toward A. Repeat for three rows.

Figure 5
Join 3 blocks and 4 A pieces to make a row.

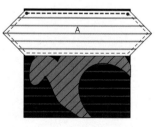

Figure 6
Stop stitching at the marked
dots on each A piece.

Step 4. Sew a B triangle to the top outside edge of each row as shown in Figure 7, stopping stitching at the marked dots on each piece; press seams toward A.

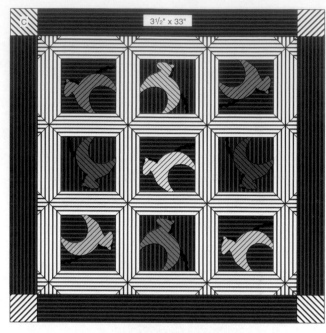

Zebra Kid's Quilt
Placement Diagram
40" x 40"

Figure 7
Sew a B triangle to the top
outside edge of each row.

Step 5. Join the three rows with A pieces as in Step 3; press seams toward A.

Step 6. Arrange the remaining A and B pieces at the top and bottom of the pieced section referring to the Placement Diagram; sew B pieces to A pieces as in Step 4.

Step 7. Sew the A-B units to the top and bottom edges to complete the pieced center.

Step 8. Sew a 4" x 33½" magenta subtle stripe border strip cut in Step 4 of Making Zebra Blocks to opposite sides of the completed center. Press seams toward strips.

Step 9. Sew a C square to each end of the remaining two strips; sew to the top and bottom of the pieced center. Press seams toward strips.

Finishing the Quilt

Step 1. Sandwich batting between the completed top and prepared backing piece; pin or baste layers together to hold flat for quilting.

Step 2. Quilt as desired by hand or machine. *Note: The quilt shown was hand-quilted along the edge of the stripes in each A and B piece as shown in Figure 8 and around each zebra shape using magenta hand-quilting thread.*

Step 3. When quilting is complete, trim batting and backing even with quilted top; remove pins or basting.

Step 4. Join the 2¼"-wide magenta-and-white strips cut in Step 4 for Making Zebra Blocks on short ends to make one long strip for binding.

Step 5. Fold the binding strip in half along length with wrong sides together; press.

Step 6. Bind edges to finish. ❖

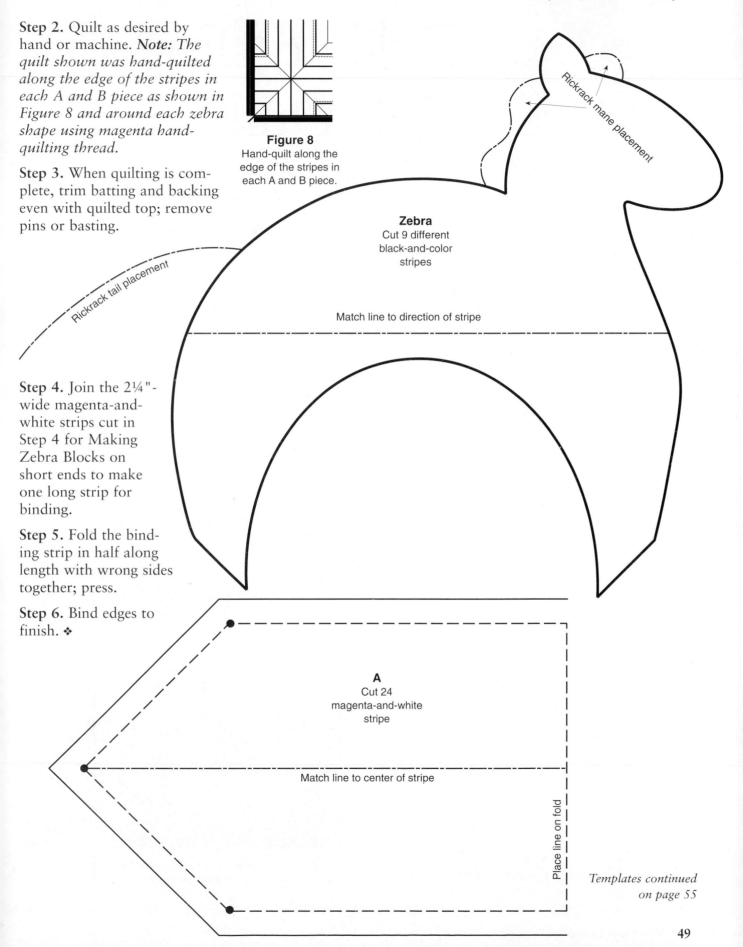

Figure 8
Hand-quilt along the edge of the stripes in each A and B piece.

Rickrack mane placement

Zebra
Cut 9 different black-and-color stripes

Match line to direction of stripe

Rickrack tail placement

A
Cut 24 magenta-and-white stripe

Match line to center of stripe

Place line on fold

Templates continued on page 55

Teddy & Friends Wall Quilt

By Marian Shenk

Animal designs make perfect appliqué shapes for a child's wall quilt.

Quick-Bias Covered Seams

Use HeatnBond Lite iron-on adhesive to apply animal and heart shapes to background blocks. After joining the blocks, cover seams with Clover Quick Bias Tape, a narrow bias ready to fuse in place and available on an 11-yard roll. Unique Stitch fabric glue is used to apply ribbon, bows and eyes to project.

Project Specifications

Skill Level: Intermediate
Quilt Size: 20½" x 25½"

Materials

- 5" x 5" scrap orange solid for duck bill and feet
- 1 (5" x 5") square each navy, green and gold solids for hearts
- 2 rectangles each 5½" x 8" navy, green and gold solids for block backgrounds
- Scraps white, gold, brown and tan velour for animal appliqués
- ½ yard red print for center strip and borders
- Batting 26" x 31"
- Backing 26" x 31"
- Neutral color and navy all-purpose thread
- Black machine-embroidery thread
- Cream hand-quilting thread
- Brown 6-strand embroidery floss
- 1 roll navy Clover Quick Bias Tape
- 1 package navy wide bias tape
- Scraps of yellow, green, red and blue satin ribbon
- ½ yard HeatnBond Lite iron-on adhesive
- Unique Stitch fabric glue
- 10 (¼") eyes
- Basic sewing tools and supplies and water-erasable marker or pencil

Teddy & Friends Wall Quilt
Placement Diagram
20½" x 25½"

Teddy & Friends Wall Quilt

Step 4. Cut four 5¼" pieces of navy quick bias; center and fuse over seams between rectangles on side strips. Stitch on each edge of the quick bias using navy all-purpose thread as shown in Figure 2.

Figure 2
Stitch on each edge
of the quick bias.

Step 5. Cut two 23" lengths of navy quick bias; center and press over seams between A panel and strips and stitch as in Step 4.

Step 6. Trace the animal and heart shapes on the paper side of the iron-on adhesive. Cut out shapes, leaving a margin around each one. *Note: Shapes have been reversed for fusible machine appliqué.*

Step 7. Fuse shapes to the wrong side of fabric scraps as directed on each piece for color; cut out shapes on traced lines. Remove paper backing. Transfer all detail lines to cut-out shapes using a water-erasable marker or pencil.

Step 8. Center and fuse the dog to the upper green rectangle, the duck to the upper navy rectangle, the bunny to the lower navy rectangle and the kitty to the lower green rectangle. Fuse the bear with foot 3" up from the bottom edge of A at an angle referring to Figure 3 for positioning.

Step 9. Fuse the heart shapes above the bear, centering the gold heart 6½" above bear's arms, the navy heart approximately 3" above arms and angled toward gold side rectangle and the green heart approximately 1½" above ear, again referring to Figure 3.

Step 10. Measure and cut pieces of narrow satin ribbon in a variety of colors to fit from bear's arm to bottom of heart shapes. Apply a bead of fabric

Completing the Quilt Top

Step 1. Cut an 8" x 23" rectangle red print for center A panel.

Step 2. Sew a gold solid rectangle between a green and navy solid rectangle on the 5½" edges to make a strip; repeat for two strips. Press seams toward darker fabrics.

Step 3. Sew the A panel between the two pieced strips as shown in Figure 1 to complete the pieced background.

5½"
x 8"

Figure 1
Sew the A panel between
the 2 pieced shapes.

Figure 3
Arrange pieces as shown.

bottom border strips. Do not stitch over these strips after fusing.

Finishing the Quilt

Step 1. Sandwich batting between the completed top and prepared backing piece; pin or baste layers together to hold flat for quilting.

Step 2. Quilt as desired by hand or machine. *Note: The quilt shown was hand-quilted around each appliqué shape and using the patterns given using cream hand-quilting thread.*

Step 3. When quilting is complete, trim batting and backing even with quilted top; remove pins or basting.

Step 4. Bind edges using navy wide bias tape to finish.

Step 5. Apply a dot of fabric glue to the backside of each ¼" eye; place on animals as marked on patterns to finish. ❖

glue to the wrong side of each ribbon piece and glue in place. Let dry.

Step 11. Using black machine-embroidery thread and a medium-width machine zigzag-stitch, stitch around each appliqué shape and on detail lines.

Step 12. Using 3 strands brown embroidery floss, satin-stitch the kitty, bear and dog's nose. Add mouth and whiskers to kitty using a stem stitch.

Step 13. Make small ribbon bows from narrow satin ribbon. Apply a dot of fabric glue to the center of each bow and apply to the base of each heart and at the neck of the dog, kitty, duck, and bunny shapes.

Step 14. Cut two strips each 2" x 21" and 2" x 26" red print. Sew the shorter strips to the top and bottom and longer strips to opposite sides of the completed center, mitering corners. Trim corner miters to ¼"; press open. Press border seams toward strips.

Step 15. Cut two each 21" and 26" strips navy quick bias. Pin and apply the 26" pieces to cover the seams of the long border strips first and then the 21" pieces to cover the seams of the top and

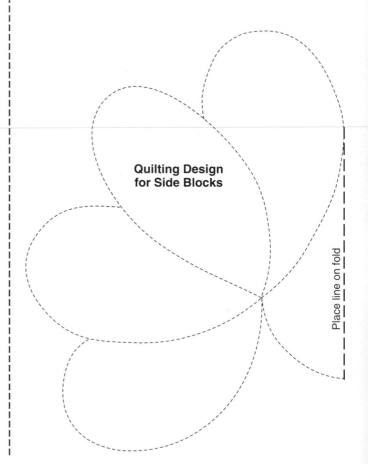

Quilting Design for Side Blocks

Place line on fold

Quilting Design for Bear Center

Place line on fold

Heart
Cut 1 each navy, gold & green solids

Teddy
Cut 1 brown velour

Quilting Design for Borders

Dog
Cut 1 tan velour

Bunny
Cut 1 white velour

Kitty
Cut 1 tan velour

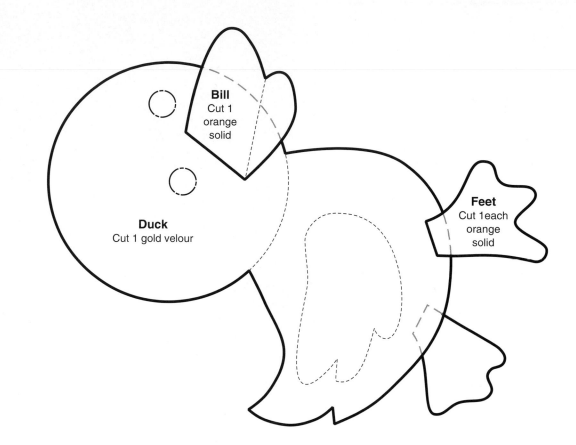

Bill
Cut 1
orange
solid

Duck
Cut 1 gold velour

Feet
Cut 1 each
orange
solid

Zebra Kid's Quilt

Continued from page 49

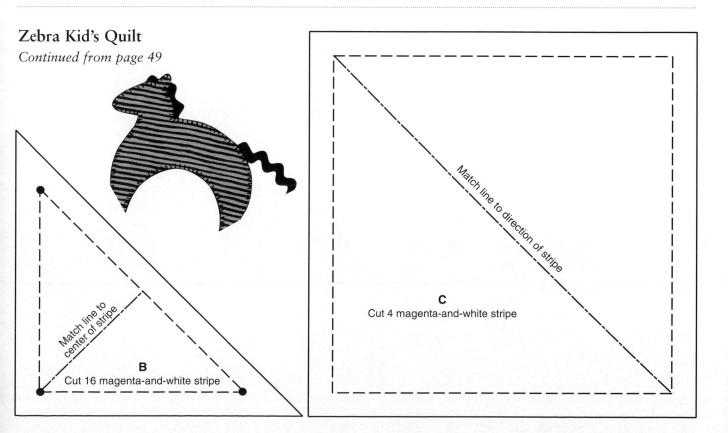

Match line to
center of stripe

B
Cut 16 magenta-and-white stripe

Match line to direction of stripe

C
Cut 4 magenta-and-white stripe

Home for Christmas

Holiday Kitchen Cheer

By Julie Weaver

Create some holiday cheer using fabrics from your scrap bag and quick fusible-appliqué techniques.

Kitchen Towels

Project Specifications
Skill Level: Beginner
Towel Size: 20" x 28"

Materials
- 3 (20" x 28") cotton kitchen towels
- Light, medium and dark green, blue, gold, orange, brown, tan and cream scraps
- Black all-purpose or machine-embroidery thread
- Brown 6-strand embroidery floss
- ½ yard Lite Steam-A-Seam 2 double-stitch fusible web
- The Appliqué Pressing Sheet
- Permanent black and orange fine-tip markers
- 4 (¼") navy blue buttons

- Basic sewing tools and supplies and water-erasable marker or pencil

Instructions

Note: Appliqué motifs are given in reverse for fusible appliqué.

Step 1. Referring to the full-size patterns given for each snowman motif, trace shapes onto the paper side of the fusible web. Remember to add extra where pieces overlap one another. Cut out shapes, leaving a margin around each one.

Step 2. Referring to manufacturer's instructions and colors listed on patterns, bond fusible shapes to the wrong side of selected scraps.

Step 3. Cut out shapes on traced lines; remove paper backing. Stack shapes by motif.

Step 4. Place the appliqué pressing sheet over the printed design; arrange pieces in place on the sheet in numerical order, layering as necessary, to create one snowman motif. Move the pressing sheet to ironing board without disturbing pieces; iron shapes in place on the pressing sheet.

Step 5. Transfer the appliqué motif in one piece 2¼" from the bottom of the center of a 20" x 28" cotton kitchen towel as shown in Figure 1; adjust, if necessary and iron in place. Repeat for three snowman motifs.

Step 6. Using a machine blanket or satin stitch and black all-purpose or

Figure 1
Center motif on kitchen towel 2¼" from bottom.

machine-embroidery thread, stitch around each fused shape.

Step 7. Referring to patterns, draw in facial features on each snowman using permanent fine-tip markers using black for eyes and mouths and orange for noses.

Step 8. Sew ¼" navy blue buttons to Snowman Motifs 1 and 3 as indicated on patterns for positioning.

Step 9. Transfer arm embroidery detail lines to fused motifs using a water-erasable marker or pencil and referring to the patterns.

Step 10. Chain-stitch stick arms on snowmen using 3 strands brown embroidery floss referring to Figure 2.

Snowman Towel 1
Placement Diagram
20" x 28"

Snowman Towel 2
Placement Diagram
20" x 28"

Snowman Towel 3
Placement Diagram
20" x 28"

Figure 2
Make a chain stitch as shown.

Caroling, Caroling Wall Quilt

Project Specifications
Skill Level: Intermediate
Quilt Size: 20" x 24"

Materials
- Scraps white, cream, tan, brown, green, red, blue and orange prints, plaids or tone-on-tones for appliqué
- ¼ yard tan plaid
- 1 yard navy blue sky print

Caroling, Caroling Wall Quilt
Placement Diagram
20" x 24"

- Backing 26" x 30"
- Batting 26" x 30"
- All-purpose thread to match fabrics
- Black machine-embroidery thread
- Navy blue quilting thread
- Brown 6-strand embroidery floss
- ¼ yard Lite Steam-A-Seam 2 double-stick fusible web
- The Appliqué Pressing Sheet
- Black permanent fine-tip marker
- 3 each ¼" navy blue, black and green buttons
- Basic sewing tools and supplies

Completing the Top

Note: Appliqué motifs are given in reverse for fusible appliqué.

Step 1. Cut a 12½" x 16½" rectangle navy blue sky print for background.

Step 2. Trace the snow pattern given onto the paper side of the fusible web, making complete pattern as shown in Figure 3; cut out shape, leaving a margin all around. Remove paper liner; fuse to the wrong side of a white scrap. Cut out shape on traced lines; remove paper backing.

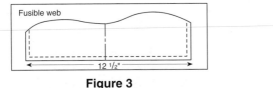

Figure 3
Make a complete pattern of
the snow piece as shown.

Step 3. Position and fuse the snow piece to bottom edge of the background rectangle, matching corners.

Step 4. Cut two 2" x 16½" A strips and two 2" x 15½" B strips tan plaid. Sew A to opposite sides and B to the top and bottom of the background; press seams toward strips.

Step 5. Cut two 1½" x 19½" C strips and two 1½" x 17½" D strips navy blue sky print. Sew C to opposite sides and D to the top and bottom of the background; press seams toward strips.

Step 6. Cut two 2" x 21½" E strips and two 2" x 20½" F strips tan plaid. Sew E to opposite sides and F to the top and bottom of the background; press seams toward strips.

Step 7. Prepare pattern pieces for appliqué as in Steps 1–4 for Kitchen Towels and referring to the full-size pattern given for snowmen motif.

Step 8. Center Snowman 2 on pieced top 2" up from bottom edge of snow piece. Place Snowman 1 and tree under the left side of Snowman 2 and Snowman 3 under the right side referring to the Placement Diagram for positioning; adjust, if necessary and iron in place.

Step 9. Using a machine blanket or satin stitch and black machine-embroidery thread, stitch around each fused shape.

Step 10. Referring to patterns, draw in facial features on each snowman using black permanent fine-tip marker.

Step 11. Sew ¼" navy blue buttons to Snowman 1, ¼" black buttons to Snowman 2 and ¼" green buttons to Snowman 3 as indicated on patterns for positioning.

Step 12. Transfer arm embroidery detail lines to fused motifs using a water-erasable marker or pencil and referring to the patterns.

Step 13. Chain-stitch stick arms on snowmen using 3 strands brown embroidery floss referring to Figure 2 on page 59.

Step 14. Prepare star motifs for appliqué as for snowmen. Arrange on the stitched top referring to the Placement Diagram for positioning; fuse in place.

Step 15. Stitch Star shapes in place as in Step 12.

Finishing the Quilt

Step 1. Sandwich batting between the completed top and prepared backing piece; pin or baste layers together to hold flat for quilting.

Step 2. Quilt as desired by hand or machine. *Note: The quilt shown was machine-quilted in the background and in C and D border strips using a meandering design, around snowmen and in the ditch of border seams using quilting thread to match fabric.*

Step 3. When quilting is complete, trim batting and backing even with quilted top; remove pins or basting.

Step 4. Cut three 2¼" by fabric width strips navy

blue sky print. Join strips on short ends to make one long strip for binding.

Step 5. Fold the binding strip in half along length

with wrong sides together; press. Bind edges to finish. ❖

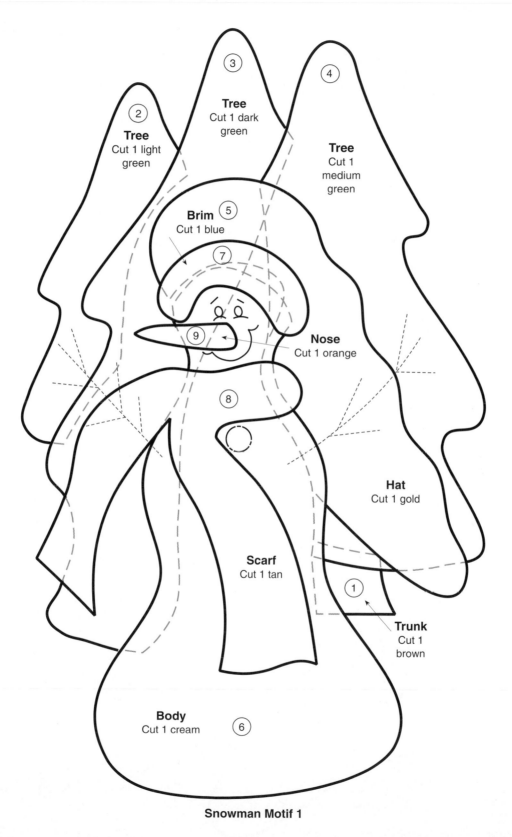

Snowman Motif 1

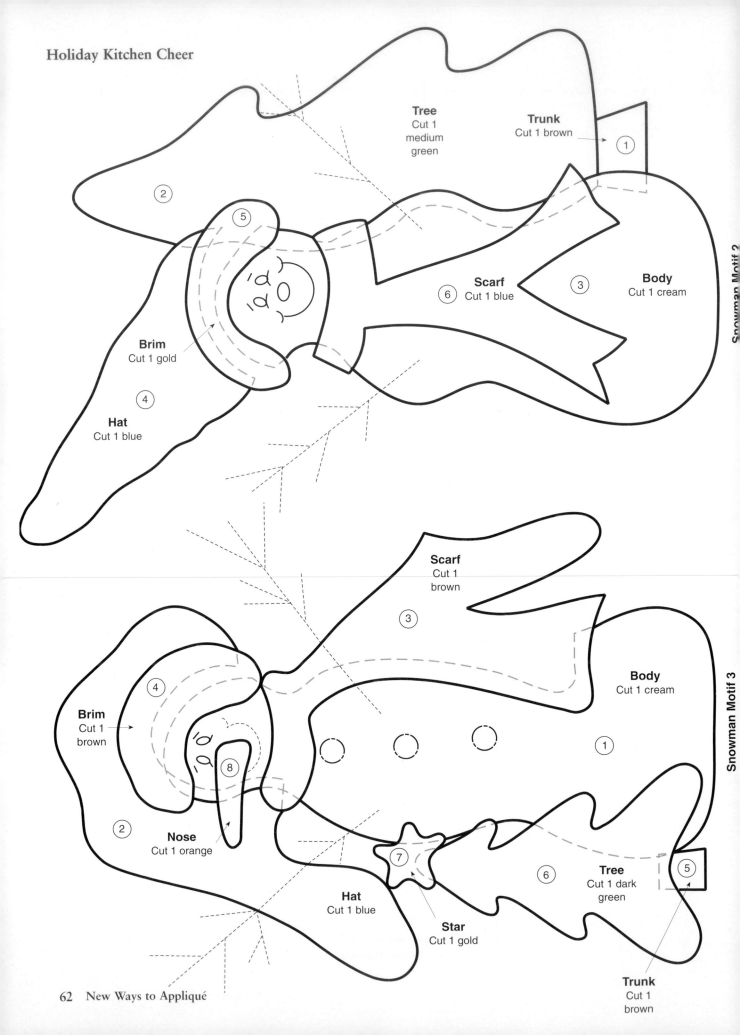

Holiday Kitchen Cheer

Tree
Cut 1
medium
green

Trunk
Cut 1 brown

②

①

⑤

Body
Cut 1 cream

③

Scarf
Cut 1 blue

⑥

Brim
Cut 1 gold

④

Hat
Cut 1 blue

Snowman Motif 2

Scarf
Cut 1
brown

③

Body
Cut 1 cream

①

Brim
Cut 1
brown

④

②

⑧

Nose
Cut 1 orange

Hat
Cut 1 blue

⑦

Star
Cut 1 gold

⑤

Tree
Cut 1 dark
green

⑥

Trunk
Cut 1
brown

Snowman Motif 3

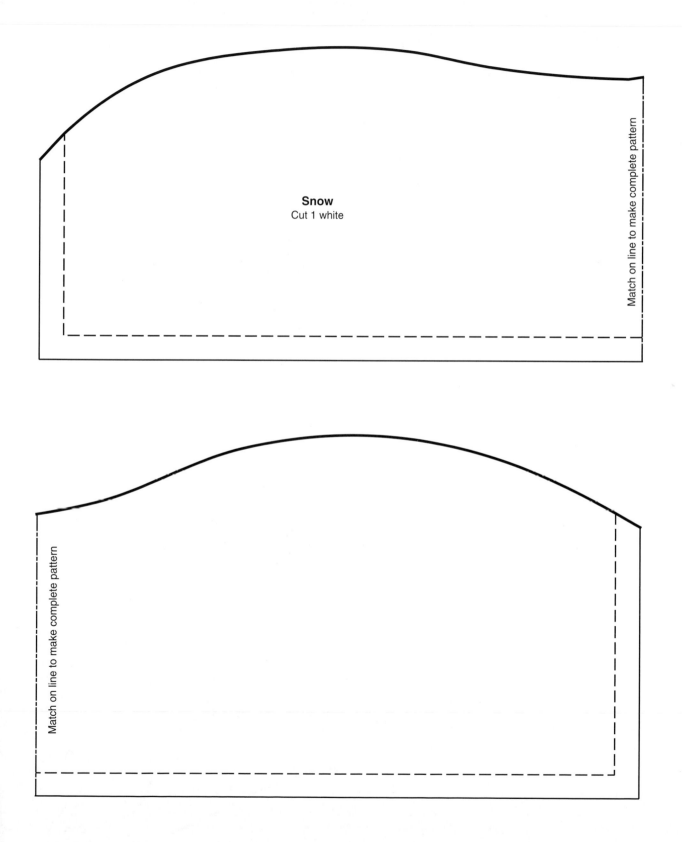

Snow
Cut 1 white

Match on line to make complete pattern

Match on line to make complete pattern

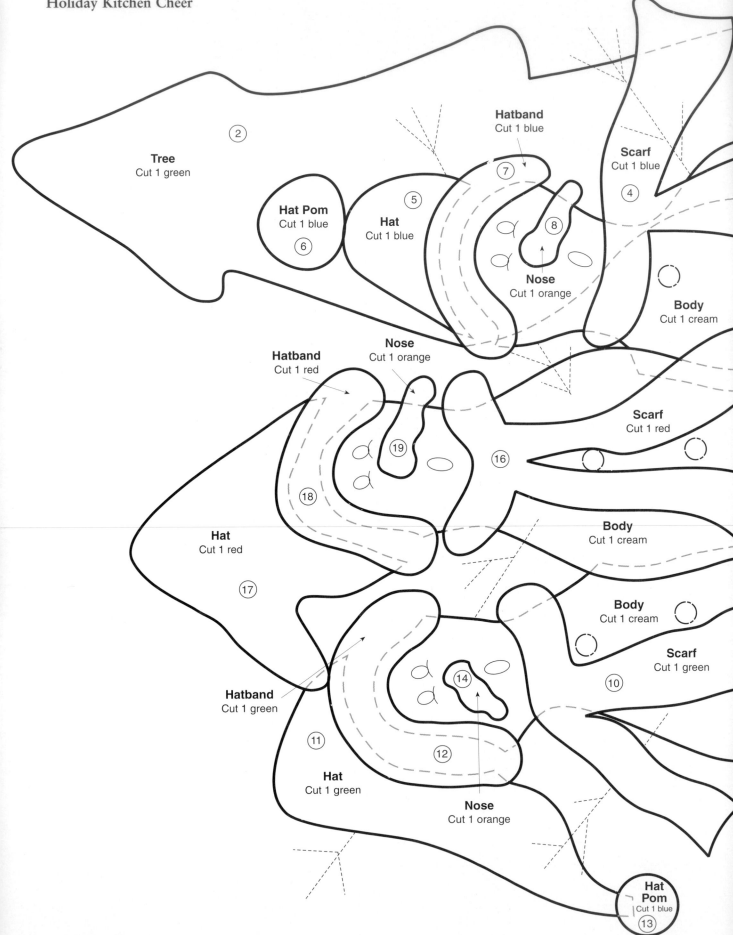

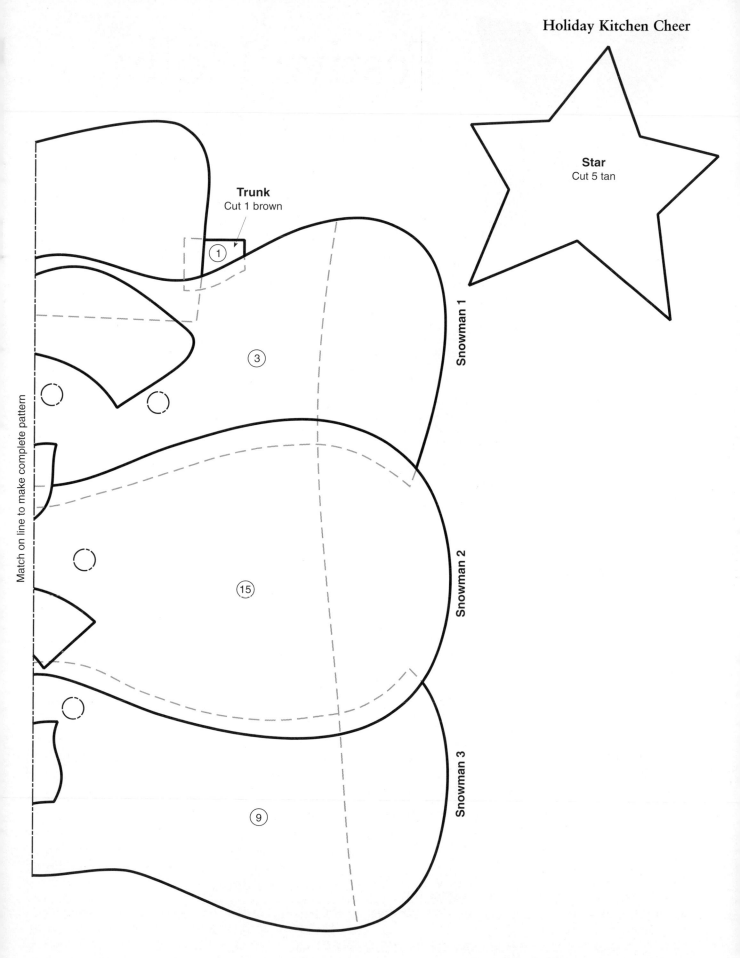

Star
Cut 5 tan

Trunk
Cut 1 brown

①

③

Snowman 1

Match on line to make complete pattern

⑮

Snowman 2

Snowman 3

⑨

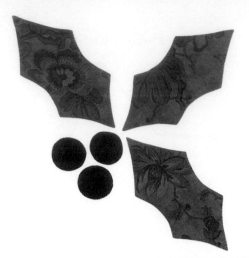

Festive Holly Table Cover

By Julie Weaver

A subtle pieced-center background is the perfect showcase for the appliqué holly leaf motifs.

Combination Piecing & Appliqué

A double-stick fusible web was used to bond the holly leaves and berries to the pieced background, which is made with triangles of assorted white and cream-on-cream prints.

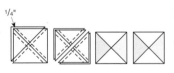

Project Specifications

Skill Level: Beginner
Quilt Size: 40" x 40"

Materials

- 36 (5¼" x 5¼") squares assorted white, off-white and cream tone-on-tones
- ¼ yard green tone-on-tone
- ⅔ yard red tone-on-tone
- 1 yard red-and-cream stripe
- Backing 46" x 46"
- Batting 46" x 46"
- All-purpose thread to match fabrics
- Cream and burgundy quilting thread
- ½ yard Lite Steam-A-Seam 2 double-stick fusible web
- Basic sewing tools and supplies

Completing the Top

Step 1. With right sides together arrange the assorted white, off-white and cream tone-on-tone background squares into 18 pairs.

Step 2. Draw a diagonal line from corner to corner on one side of each pair as shown in Figure 1.

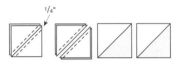

Figure 1
Draw a diagonal line from corner to corner on 1 side of each pair.

Figure 2
Sew ¼" on each side of the drawn line; cut on the drawn line to make half-square triangles.

Step 3. Sew ¼" on each side of the drawn line; cut on the drawn line to make 36 half-square triangles referring to Figure 2.

Step 4. Arrange the half-square triangles into 18 pairs, making sure there are different fabrics in each pair. With right sides together and opposing seams, draw a diagonal line from corner to corner on one side of each pair as shown in Figure 3.

Figure 3
Draw a diagonal line from corner to corner on 1 side of each pair.

Figure 4
Sew ¼" on each side of the drawn line; cut on the drawn line to make quarter-square units.

Step 5. Sew ¼" on each side of the drawn line; cut on the drawn line and press referring to Figure 4 to make 36 quarter-square triangle units.

Step 6. Arrange the quarter-square triangle units in six rows of six blocks each. Join blocks in rows; press seams in one direction. Join rows with seams or rows going in opposite directions to reduce bulk to complete the pieced center. Press seams in one direction.

Step 7. Cut two 1½" x 24½" A strips and two 1½" x 26½" B strips red tone-on-tone. Sew A to

opposite sides and B to the top and bottom of the pieced center; press seams toward strips.

Step 8. Cut four 7" by fabric width strips red-and-cream stripe. Center and sew a strip to each side of the pieced center, placing a stripe at the center of each side and stopping stitching ¼" from each end; miter corners, matching stripes. Trim seam to ¼"; press seam open.

Step 9. Cut four 1" by fabric width strips red tone-on-tone. Sew a strip to opposite sides of the pieced top; press and trim excess strips at each end. Sew the remaining strips to the top and bottom of the quilt; press and trim excess strips at each end.

Step 10. Trace appliqué shapes onto one paper side of the fusible web using patterns given, tracing 12 each berries and leaves.

Step 11. Cut out shapes, leaving a margin around each one. Remove unmarked paper side of each shape; fuse to the wrong side of the fabrics as directed on patterns.

Step 12. Cut out shapes on traced lines; remove paper backing.

Step 13. Arrange three leaves and three berries at each corner referring to Figure 5 for placement; fuse in place.

Step 14. Machine buttonhole-stitch around each shape using matching all-purpose thread.

Finishing the Quilt

Step 1. Sandwich batting between the completed top and prepared backing piece; pin or baste layers together to hold flat for quilting.

Step 2. Quilt as desired by hand or machine. *Note: The quilt shown was machine-quilted in the background in a meandering design and in the ditch of border seams using cream quilting thread and on the stripe border and in the seam between the border strips using burgundy quilting thread.*

Step 3. When quilting is complete, trim batting and backing even with quilted top; remove pins or basting.

Step 4. Cut four 2¼" by fabric width strips red

Festive Holly Table Cover
Placement Diagram
40" x 40"

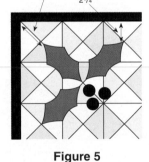

Figure 5
Arrange leaves and berries at corners as shown.

tone-on-tone. Join strips on short ends to make one long strip for binding.

Step 5. Fold the binding strip in half along length with wrong sides together; press.

Step 6. Bind edges referring to the General Instructions. ❖

Leaf
Cut 12 green tone-on-tone

Berry
Cut 12 red tone-on-tone

Snowman Tree Skirt

By Chris Malone

Make perfect curved appliqué shapes for hand appliqué using a few household products.

Freezer Paper Appliqué

Freezer paper and spray starch used in the preparation of the curved appliqué shapes help make the edges smooth and the stitching quick and easy.

Project Specifications

Skill Level: Intermediate
Quilt Size: 41½" diameter

Materials

- ⅛ yard orange mottled flannel
- ⅙ yard multicolored plaid flannel
- ¼ yard red print flannel
- ½ yard off-white solid flannel
- 1¼ yards cotton batting
- 2½ yards medium blue mottled flannel
- All-purpose thread to match fabrics
- Medium brown, black, yellow and ecru 6-strand embroidery floss
- 4 yards red jumbo rickrack
- 1 yard ⅞"-wide red grosgrain ribbon
- 12 (¼") black buttons
- 8 (1") black buttons
- 8 (⅞") black buttons
- 7 (¾") yellow buttons

- 34 (½"–¾") white buttons
- Spray starch
- No-fray solution
- Fabri-Tac Permanent Adhesive
- Basic sewing tools and supplies, double sheet newspaper, string, freezer paper, paintbrush, air-soluble pen

Completing the Top

Step 1. To make pattern for tree skirt, fold the newspaper in quarters as shown in Figure 1. *The paper should be at least 44" square.*

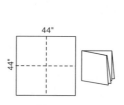

Figure 1
Fold newspaper in quarters as shown.

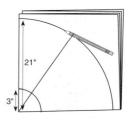

Figure 2
Mark lines on paper with string and pencil as shown.

Step 2. Tie one end of the string to a pencil and measure 21" from tied end. Hold this point at the folded corner of the paper and swing the pencil from one edge of the paper to the other side, marking a quarter-circle on the paper with pencil lines as shown in Figure 2.

Step 3. Repeat Step 2, marking another line with string only 3" to mark opening circle, again referring to Figure 2.

Step 4. Cut out paper pattern on the marked lines; skirt should measure 18" between edge and the 6" center opening.

Step 5. Cut a straight line from the inner circle to the outer circle for skirt opening in back.

Step 6. Using the newspaper pattern, cut two medium blue mottled flannel and one batting.

Step 7. Trace eight of each snowman shape and seven hearts onto the dull side of the freezer paper.

Step 8. Place the shiny side of the freezer paper on the wrong side of the appliqué fabrics; iron in place with a dry iron.

Step 9. Cut around the freezer-paper shapes, adding a generous ¼" seam allowance all around each shapes.

Step 10. Fold the seam allowance over the edge of the freezer paper; hand-baste through the fabric and paper, checking the right sides of the shapes often to be sure curved lines are smooth; press with a dry iron.

Step 11. Spray a small amount of liquid starch

into a small container such as a jar lid. Dip the paintbrush into the starch and apply to part of the seam allowance; press with iron point until set. Repeat all around appliqué. ***Note:*** *Adding spray starch to seam allowance makes the appliqué easy to work with and helps maintain the smooth curves while sewing.*

Step 12. Remove basting stitches and freezer paper.

Step 13. Place the appliqué shapes on the flannel tree skirt with snowman 4" from each edge of skirt back opening, alternating snowmen and heart shapes. The bottom of each snowman is 2¼" from bottom of skirt and tip of heart is 3¼" from bottom of skirt. Pin appliqué shapes in place; sew to skirt with small appliqué stitch with matching all-purpose thread.

Step 14. Sew scarf to neck and nose to head of

each snowman, alternating nose position in various poses from straight up, straight down and off to each side referring to the Placement Diagram.

Step 15. Cut a 1¾" circle from paper using pattern given for smile. Use the air-soluble pen to draw a smile on each snowman, with a full smile on the faces with noses pointing up and a partial smile (coming up from under scarf) on remaining snowmen. Backstitch smile with 2 strands of black embroidery floss.

Step 16. Sew two ¼" black buttons to face for eyes. *Note: Snowmen with noses pointing up do not have eyes.*

Step 17. Use air-soluble pen to draw twig arms about 2¾" long on each side of snowmen with tips crossing edge of adjacent hearts. Backstitch arms with 4 strands of medium brown floss.

Step 18. Baste red jumbo rickrack along bottom edge of skirt by sewing center of rickrack over the ¼" seam line as shown in Figure 3.

Figure 3
Center and baste the rickrack
over the ¼" seam line.

Step 19. Cut ribbon in half and tack one end of each ribbon to each side of back opening at top even with edge of skirt; sew ¼" from edge as shown in Figure 4.

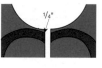

Figure 4
Sew ¼" from edge.

Finishing the Tree Skirt

Step 1. Layer and pin the skirt pieces together with batting on bottom, backing on top with right side up and appliquéd skirt top right side down. Sew all around skirt with ¼" seam, leaving a 12" opening along one straight edge of back opening.

Step 2. Clip curves, trim corners and turn right side out through opening. Fold seam allowance in on opening and hand-stitch opening closed. Press and topstitch close to edge as shown in Figure 5.

Figure 5
Topstitch close to edge.

Step 3. Cut eight 1" x 6" strips multicolored plaid flannel for scarf ends.

Step 4. Pull threads to fringe ½" at each end of each strip; apply no-fray solution to long edges and let dry.

Snowman Tree Skirt

Step 5. Tie a knot in the center of each strip. Using Fabri-Tac Permanent Adhesive, glue knot of scarf ends to scarf, varying the placement from each side to the center referring to the Placement Diagram for positioning suggestions.

Step 6. Add buttons to skirt by sewing through all layers using 3 strands matching embroidery floss, sewing 1" and ⅞" black buttons to each snowman body; yellow button to center of each heart and white buttons randomly above and around appliqué shapes to simulate snowflakes. ❖

Snowman Tree Skirt
Placement Diagram
41½" Diameter

Heart
Cut 7 red print flannel

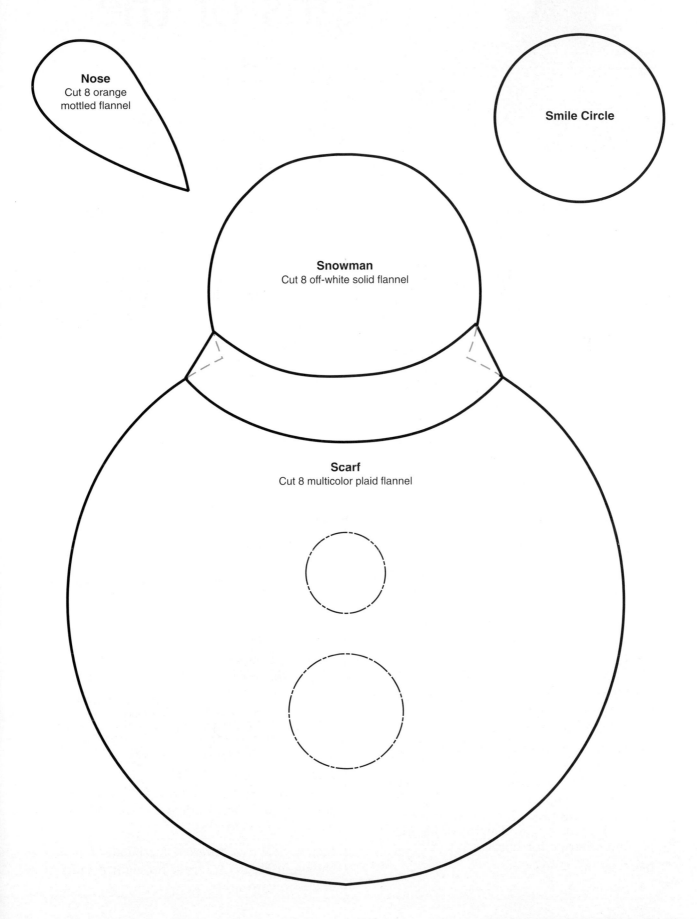

Nose
Cut 8 orange
mottled flannel

Smile Circle

Snowman
Cut 8 off-white solid flannel

Scarf
Cut 8 multicolor plaid flannel

Signs of the Seasons

By Marian Shenk

A pieced wreath design is surrounded by motifs cut from a large Christmas print.

Project Specifications
Skill Level: Beginner
Quilt Size: 30" x 30"
Block Size: 12" x 12"
Number of Blocks: 1

Materials
- 1 (3" x 36") bias strip red-and-green plaid for bow
- Fat quarters of 3 different green-with-gold prints for leaves and block piecing
- ⅓ yard red print for binding
- ½ yard Christmas print with large poinsettias
- 1 yard cream-with-gold print for background and block piecing
- 1 yard red-and-green border stripe (need four 3½"-wide by 36" lengths of identical portion of stripe for borders)
- Backing 36" x 36"
- Batting 36" x 36"

- Green and red machine-embroidery thread
- Cream quilting thread
- All-purpose thread to match fabrics and buttons
- ½ yard HeatnBond Lite fusible web
- ¾ yard fabric stabilizer
- 12 (⅜") red buttons
- 7 (⅜") gold jingle bells
- Basic sewing tools and supplies

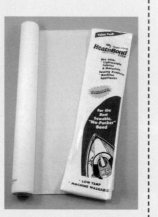

Wreath
12" x 12" Block

Piecing the Top

Step 1. Assign numbers to each green-with-gold print.

Step 2. To make the Wreath block, cut two 5¼" x 5¼" squares each of green-with-gold prints 1 and 2. Cut each square in half on both diagonals to make A triangles as shown in Figure 1.

Figure 1
Cut each 5¼" x 5¼" square in half on both diagonals to make A triangles.

Figure 2
Cut each 4⅞" x 4⅞" square in half on 1 diagonal to make B triangles.

Step 3. Cut two 4⅞" x 4⅞" squares each green-with-gold 1 and cream-with-gold prints. Cut each square in half on one diagonal to make B triangles as shown in Figure 2.

Step 4. Sew two different A triangles together as shown in Figure 3; repeat for eight A units. Press seams toward fabric 2.

Figure 3
Join 2 different
A triangles.

Figure 4
Join 2 A units.

Step 5. Join two A units as shown in Figure 4; repeat for four units. Press seams in one direction.

Step 6. Sew a cream-with-gold print B to a green-with-gold print B to make a B unit as shown in Figure 5; repeat for four B units. Press seams toward darker fabric.

Figure 5
Sew a cream-with-gold
print B to a green-with-gold
print B to make a B unit.

Step 7. Cut one 4½" x 4½" square cream-with-gold print for C.

Step 8. Sew an A unit between two B units as shown in Figure 6; repeat for two units. Press seams toward B units.

Figure 6
Sew an A unit between 2 B units.

Step 9. Sew C between two A units as shown in Figure 7; press seams away from A.

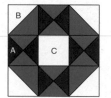

Figure 8
Sew the A-C-A unit between 2 B-A-B
units to complete the Wreath block.

Figure 7
Sew C between 2 A units.

Step 10. Sew the A-C-A unit between two B-A-B units to complete the Wreath block as shown in Figure 8; press seams away from the block center.

Step 11. Cut two 9⅜" x 9⅜" squares cream-with-gold print for D; cut each D square in half on one diagonal to make D triangles.

Step 12. Sew D to each side of the pieced block as shown in Figure 9; press seams toward D.

Step 13. Cut two 12⅞" x 12⅞" squares cream-with-gold print for E. Cut each E square in half on one diagonal to make E triangles.

Figure 9
Sew a D triangle to each
side of the pieced unit.

Step 14. Sew an E triangle to each side of the pieced unit as shown in Figure 10 to complete the pieced center.

Step 15. Cut four identical strips red-and-green stripe 3½" x 36". Mark the center of each strip. *Note: The center should be the same motif on each strip.* Match the center of the strip with the center of the pieced center.

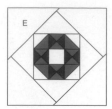

Figure 10
Sew an E triangle to each
side of the pieced unit.

Step 16. Stitch a strip to each side of the pieced center, stopping stitching ¼" from each end. Miter corner seams as shown in Figure 11; trim excess seam allowance and press seams open. *Note: Each corner should form the same design where stripe sections meet. Strips are cut a bit longer than needed to make stitching mitered seam easier.*

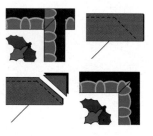

Figure 11
Miter corner seams as shown.

Appliquéing the Top

Step 1. Isolate four poinsettia motifs on the Christmas print. Measure motifs and cut squares of fusible web to fit behind them. Fuse the squares to the wrong side of each motif; cut out motifs. Remove paper backing.

Step 2. Place one poinsettia motif in each D triangle, slightly overlapping center Wreath block referring to the Placement Diagram for positioning; fuse in place referring to manufacturer's instructions.

Step 3. Trace 12 leaves on the paper side of the fusible web using pattern given; cut out shapes, leaving a margin around each one.

Step 4. Fuse shapes to the wrong sides of fabrics as directed on pattern for color; cut out shapes on traced lines. Remove paper backing.

Step 5. Arrange one leaf shape of each fabric on the E triangles 3" from corner seams as shown in

Signs of the Season
Placement Diagram
30" x 30"

Figure 12, overlapping leaves referring to lines on pattern for positioning. When satisfied with placement, fuse shapes in place referring to manufacturer's instructions.

Step 6. Cut fabric stabilizer pieces larger than all fused motifs; apply to the wrong side of the top referring to manufacturer's instructions.

Step 7. Using green machine-embroidery thread on leaves and leaf sections of fused motif and red machine-embroidery thread on the red poinsettia sections of the fused motifs, zigzag-stitch around each fused shape. Remove fabric stabilizer as directed by manufacturer.

Finishing the Quilt

Step 1. Sandwich batting between the completed top and prepared backing piece; pin or baste layers together to hold flat for quilting.

Step 2. Quilt as desired by hand or machine. *Note: The quilt shown was hand-quilted in 1" diagonal lines in the background, in the ditch of all seams and around appliqué shapes using cream quilting thread.*

Figure 12
Arrange leaf shapes on E triangles 3" from corner seams.

Step 3. When quilting is complete, trim batting and backing even with quilted top; remove pins or basting.

Step 4. Cut four 2¼" by fabric width strips red print. Join strips on short ends to make one long strip for binding.

Step 5. Fold the binding strip in half along length with wrong sides together; press.

Step 6. Bind edges referring to the General Instructions.

Step 7. Sew three ⅜" red buttons to the base of the leaf motifs using matching all-purpose thread.

Step 8. Fold the 3" x 36" red-and-green plaid bias strip in half with right sides together along length; cut each end at a 45-degree angle. Stitch along angled ends and length leaving a 4" opening in the center as shown in Figure 13; turn right side out. Press flat. Hand-stitch opening closed.

Figure 13
Stitch angled ends and along length of strip, leaving a 4" opening in the center.

Step 9. Tie the stitched strip into a bow; hand-stitch bow in placc in the center of the top A unit in the Wreath block.

Step 10. Hand-stitch a gold jingle bell in the center of each dark B triangle and in the center of the side and bottom A units to finish. ❖

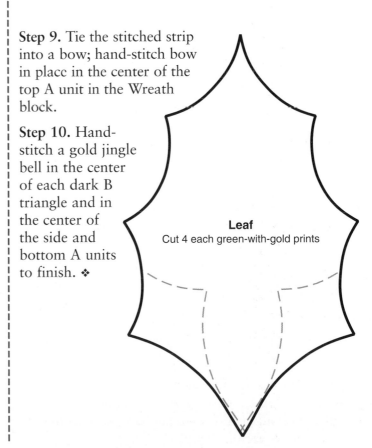

Leaf
Cut 4 each green-with-gold prints

Christmas Outlines

By Connie Kauffman

Make a simple, yet elegant Christmas table setting using appliqué outlines.

Overlapped Fusible Appliqué

Only a double-stick fusible web will work with these instructions because it has pressure sensitive adhesive on both sides of the fusible material; other fusible webs will not work.

Project Specifications
Skill Level: Beginner
Runner Size: 56" x 19"
Place Mat Size: 18" x 12"

Materials
- ⅛ yard white-with-gold print
- ¼ yard light green print
- ⅓ yard dark green print
- ⅓ yard white-with-dark-gold print
- ¾ yard gold print
- 2 yards red-with-gold print
- Hobbs Premium cotton batting 58" x 21" and 19" x 13"
- All-purpose thread to match fabrics
- 2 packages Steam-A-Seam 2 double-stick fusible web
- Sulky gold metallic thread
- Sulky KK2000 spray adhesive
- Basic sewing tools and supplies

Completing the Runner
Step 1. Cut two 56½" x 19½" rectangles red-with-gold print for runner top and backing, and a same-size batting piece.

Step 2. Fold the runner top with right sides together along length and crease to mark center. Unfold and mark a dot at the center point on each short end.

Step 3. Fold the corners to the center crease on each side of each end and press as shown in Figure 1; unfold.

Figure 1
Fold the corners to the center crease on each side of each end.

Step 4. Lay the batting piece on a flat surface. Lay the backing piece on the batting right side up. Place the creased top on top right sides together.

Step 5. Stitch all around using a ¼" seam allowance and on the creased lines to make angled ends, leaving a 4" opening on one long side. Trim excess ¼" beyond seam as shown in Figure 2.

Figure 2
Trim excess ¼" beyond seam.

Step 6. Turn right side out through opening; press seams flat. Press open edges in; hand-stitch opening closed.

Step 7. Mark the star, star point and tree outline patterns on the fusible web, marking one star, five star points, two center tree and four side tree outlines.

Step 8. Cut out ¼" from the inside and outside marked lines. Remove the unmarked paper liner and place onto the wrong side of the gold print; cut out along inside and outside lines.

Step 9. Remove remaining paper liner from fabric

pieces. Place the star outline on the white-with-dark-gold print. Finger-press the outline against the fabric. Cut out the star along the outside edge of the gold print outline as shown in Figure 3.

Figure 3
Cut out the star along
the outside edge.

Figure 4
Place white-with-dark-gold print
behind star area and dark green
print behind tree area.

Step 10. Repeat Step 9 for remaining outline pieces. For the center trees, place a small piece of white-with-dark-gold print behind the small star area at top of tree and dark green print behind the tree area as shown in Figure 4.

Step 11. Fuse the star and star point outlines in place with an iron; do not fuse the tree outlines at this time.

Step 12. Spray the back of the star and star points with spray adhesive. Position the star on the center of the stitched runner referring to the Placement Diagram for positioning.

Step 13. Place the star point pieces behind the star; machine-stitch around both sides of the gold print outlines using gold metallic thread and a zigzag stitch.

Step 14. Spray the wrong side of the tree pieces with spray adhesive. Position the tree shapes at each end of the runner, overlapping side trees on center tree as shown in Figure 5.

Figure 5
Overlap trees
as shown.

Step 15. Carefully lift up the overlapping corners of the trees. Separate the gold print outline pieces from the tree pieces and re-layer in this order: center tree on bottom, side tree, gold outline for the center tree and finally, the gold outline for the side tree on top as shown in Figure 6. When all trees are positioned, iron to fuse in place.

Step 16. Machine zigzag-stitch around both

Christmas Outlines Runner
Placement Diagram
56" x 19"

Christmas Outlines Place Mat
Placement Diagram
18" x 12"

Figure 6
Re-layer tree
corners as shown.

sides of all gold outline pieces using gold metallic thread.

Step 17. Mark the star quilting design given in open spaces on the runner. Machine-quilt in a meandering design in the center of the large star, ½" around star shape and on marked star shapes using gold metallic thread.

Completing the Place Mat

Step 1. Prepare template for place mat using pattern given. Cut as directed.

Step 2. Lay the batting piece on a flat surface. Lay one red-with-gold print piece on the batting right side up. Place the remaining red-with-gold print piece on top right sides together.

Step 3. Stitch all around using a ¼" seam allowance, leaving a 3" opening on one side.

Step 4. Turn right side out through opening; press edges flat. Press open edges in; hand-stitch opening closed.

Step 5. Prepare one center and two side tree motifs and appliqué referring to Steps 7–16 for runner and to the Placement Diagram for positioning to finish. ❖

Place line on fold

Place line on fold

Place Mat Pattern
Cut 2 red-with-gold print & 1 batting

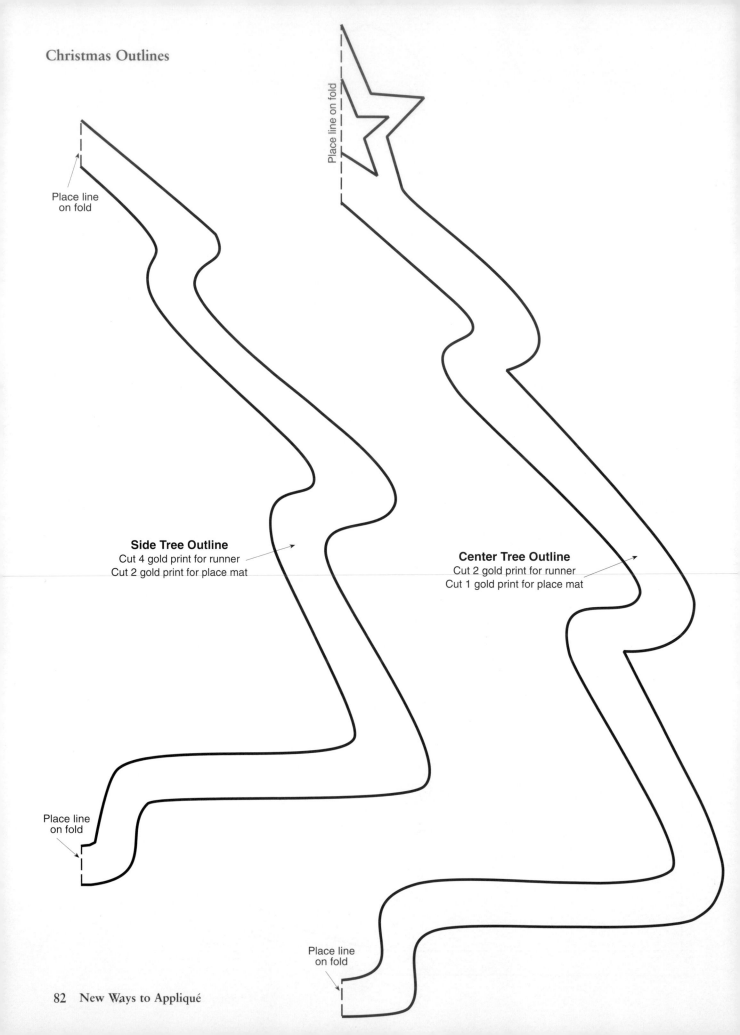

Christmas Outlines

Place line on fold

Place line on fold

Side Tree Outline
Cut 4 gold print for runner
Cut 2 gold print for place mat

Center Tree Outline
Cut 2 gold print for runner
Cut 1 gold print for place mat

Place line
on fold

Place line
on fold

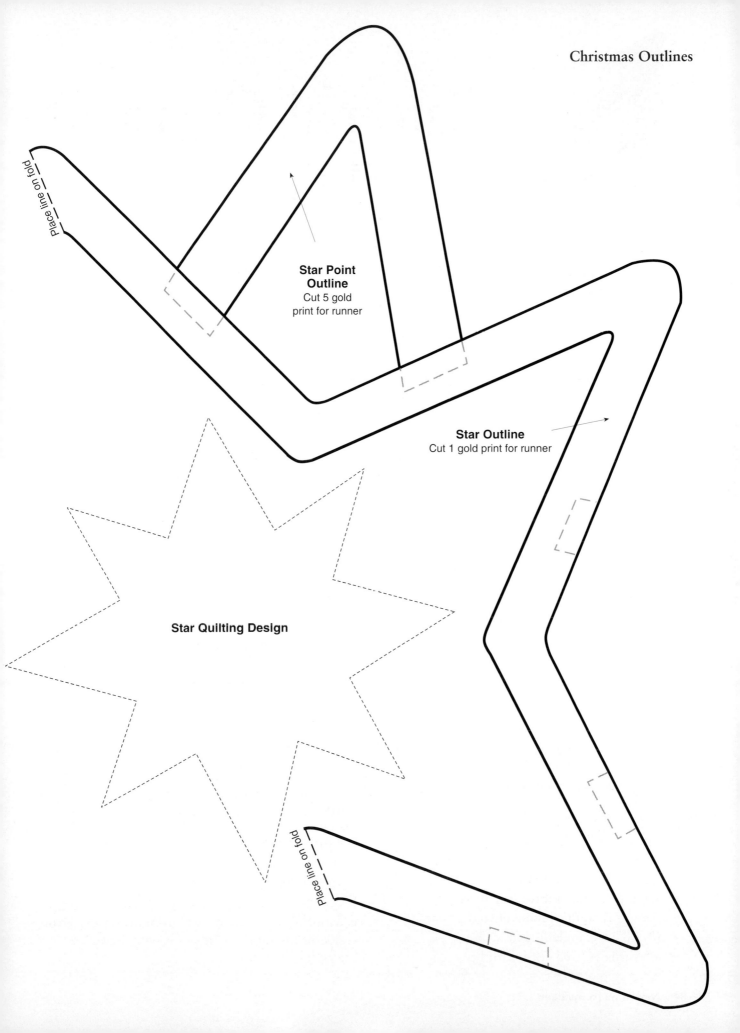

Place line on fold

**Star Point
Outline**
Cut 5 gold
print for runner

Star Outline
Cut 1 gold print for runner

Star Quilting Design

Place line on fold

Cardinal Christmas Stocking

By Barbara A. Clayton

Combine ribbon embroidery with appliqué to make this pretty Christmas stocking.

English Paper-Piecing Variation

Use paper as an accurate base to create smooth appliqué shapes. Use a pressing bar to make smooth bias strips using gold lamé.

Project Specifications
Skill Level: Advanced
Stocking Size: Approximately 8½" x 13"

Materials
- Scrap black for bird faces
- 8" x 8" piece gold lamé for beaks and tree limbs
- Scrap red solid for bird bodies
- 5" x 8" scrap medium green satin for leaves
- ⅛ yard dark green velvet for stocking cuff
- ⅓ yard off-white satin or brocade for stocking body
- ⅓ yard dark green solid for lining
- Batting 15" x 32"
- All-purpose thread to match fabrics
- Clear nylon monofilament
- Black 6-strand embroidery floss
- Green rayon machine-embroidery thread
- 5" x 8" rectangle fusible web
- 1⅔ yards ¼" red cord with lip

- 1 yard thin gold cord
- 5 yards ⅛"-wide green satin ribbon
- 2 (3mm) black beads
- 21 (4mm) red beads
- ¼" and ½" Quilter's Press Bars
- Basic sewing tools and supplies, machine zipper foot, white paper, washable fabric marker and large-eye embroidery needle

Cutting
Step 1. Trace and cut out the stocking pattern given; tape together where indicated to make the complete, full-size pattern. Cut as directed on the pattern.

Step 2. Cut two 3¾" x 13" rectangles green velvet for cuffs; repeat for one batting piece.

Step 3. Cut one 1" x 10" and one 1" x 5" bias strip gold lamé. Fold strips in half along length with wrong sides together; stitch a ¼" seam along raw edges to make tubes.

Step 4. Trim seams to ⅛". Insert the ¼" bias bar into each tube and roll the seam to the center of the bar as shown in Figure 1. Press the strips with bar inside using a cool iron; set aside.

Figure 1
Insert the ¼" bias bar into each tube and roll the seam to the center of the bar.

Appliqué Pieces
Step 1. Trace the cardinals onto white paper to make templates; cut out.

Step 2. Pin the cardinals to the red solid scrap with the right side of the cardinals on the wrong side of the fabric. Cut out leaving about ½" around each bird.

Cardinal Christmas Stocking

Step 3. Fold the fabric over the edge of the paper shapes and pin in place, clipping curves, points and inverted points referring to Figure 2. Baste along the edge of bird shapes; remove pins.

Figure 2
Fold the fabric over the edge of the paper shapes and pin in place, clipping curves, points and inverted points.

Step 4. Bond fusible web to the wrong side of the medium green satin.

Step 5. Prepare a template for the leaf shape using pattern given; trace seven leaves on the paper side of the fused fabric. Cut out on traced lines; remove paper backing.

Stocking Appliqué

Step 1. Transfer the appliqué design to the stocking front using full-size pattern and a washable fabric marker.

Step 2. Using the large-eye embroidery needle and the ⅛"-wide green satin ribbon, stitch the pine needles with long diagonal satin stitches about ¼" apart on both sides of each branch line referring to Figure 3.

Figure 3
Stitch the pine needles with long diagonal satin stitches about ¼" apart on both sides of each branch line.

Step 3. On the reverse side, fold the beginning and ending ribbon under and stitch to the back to secure.

Step 4. Arrange and hand-stitch the gold lamé bias strip branches in place as marked on stocking using clear nylon monofilament and leaving the section open on the top branch where the bird tail is tucked behind the branch.

Step 5. Arrange bird shapes, inserting tail of upper bird under gold lamé branch through the opening as shown in Figure 4; hand-stitch in place using matching all-purpose thread.

Figure 4
Insert tail of upper bird under gold lamé branch through the opening.

Step 6. Make a cut in the backside of the stocking behind each appliquéd bird as shown in Figure 5. Remove basting and paper from bird shapes.

Step 7. Prepare templates for beaks and faces; cut as directed on each piece, adding a ¼" seam allowance all around when cutting.

Step 8. Turn under seam allowance on beak and face pieces; hand-appliqué in place on birds using matching all-purpose thread.

Step 9. Hand-stitch detail lines on birds using 2 strands black embroidery floss.

Step 10. Zigzag-stitch feet over branches using black all-purpose thread referring to full-size pattern for positioning. Hand-stitch a 3mm black bead to each bird face for eyes.

Back of stocking

Figure 5
Make a cut in the backside of the stocking behind each appliquéd bird.

Stocking Assembly

Note: The stocking is stitched with a ½" seam allowance due to the ½" lip on the cord. The seam allowance is included on the pattern.

Step 1. Pin the stocking top right side up on the batting and lining layers together; baste all around near the edge of the stocking by hand or machine.

Step 2. Hand-quilt around both birds with black all-purpose thread. Hand- or machine-quilt the background area using white all-purpose thread.

Step 3. Pin the stocking back, batting and lining layers together, stitch and quilt as in Steps 1 and 2.

Step 4. Pin the red cord with lip on the edge of the stocking front, aligning lip with raw edge of front. *Note: Do not pin cord around top edge of stocking.* Machine-baste in place close to cord using a machine zipper foot as shown in Figure 6.

Step 5. Pin the stocking back to the stocking front

with right sides together; sew all around along cord basting line using the zipper foot.

Figure 6
Machine-baste in place close to cord using a machine zipper foot.

Step 6. Turn stocking right side out; smooth edges.

Step 7. Pin one of the green velvet cuff strips to the same-size batting piece.

Step 8. Pin the thin gold cord down the center of the strip making five gentle curves referring to Figure 7. Using the clear nylon monofilament in the top of the machine and all-purpose thread in the bobbin, zigzag-stitch over the cord to secure as shown in Figure 8. *Note: The cord will appear quilted.*

Figure 7
Make 5 gentle curves down the center of the cuff strip.

Figure 8
Zigzag-stitch over the cord to secure.

Figure 9
Arrange the stitched leaf shapes along the stitched cord.

Step 9. Arrange the prepared leaf shapes along the stitched cord referring to Figure 9 for positioning.

Step 10. Using only the tip of a warm iron, lightly press the leaves only, avoiding touching the velvet with the iron.

Step 11. Using green rayon machine-embroidery thread in the top of the machine and all-purpose thread in the bobbin, machine zigzag-stitch around each leaf and along vein lines on the inside of each leaf.

Step 12. Hand-stitch a cluster of three 4mm red beads at the end of each leaf next to gold cord.

Step 13. Pin the remaining red cord with lip along the bottom edge of the stitched cuff piece; stitch in place using the zipper foot and a ½" seam allowance.

Step 14. Pin the remaining green velvet cuff piece right sides together with the stitched cuff; stitch along bottom edge along cord stitching line using a ½" seam allowance as shown in Figure 10; trim seams. Finger-press seams flat.

Step 15. Pin and stitch short ends together to

make a tube using a ½" seam allowance as shown in Figure 11; finger-press seam open. Turn tube right side out.

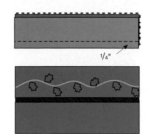

Figure 10
Stitch along bottom edge along cord stitching line using a ¼" seam allowance.

Figure 11
Pin and stitch short ends together to make a tube.

Step 16. Make a velvet loop by cutting a 1" x 5" green velvet strip. Fold with right sides together along length; stitch along length. Turn right side out through one open end. Finger-press flat with seam on side.

Step 17. Fold the stitched loop in half and pin to the top left inside seam of the stocking aligning raw ends with raw edge of stocking top.

Step 18. Pin the top right side of the velvet cuff tube to the top inside edge of the stitched stocking with tube seam centered on the back as shown in

Cardinal Christmas Stocking
Placement Diagram
Approximately 8¼" x 13"

Cardinal Christmas Stocking

Figure 12; stitch using a ½" seam allowance. Trim seam to reduce bulk.

Step 19. Pull the cuff and loop out of stocking as shown in Figure 13.

Step 20. Fold the backside raw edge of the cuff edge under ½". Pin over stitched seam as shown

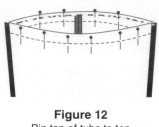

Figure 12
Pin top of tube to top

Figure 13
Pull the cuff and loop
out of stocking.

Figure 14
Pin backside edge of
cuff over stitched seam.

in Figure 14; hand-stitch in place. Fold cuff down over stocking top edge to finish. ❖

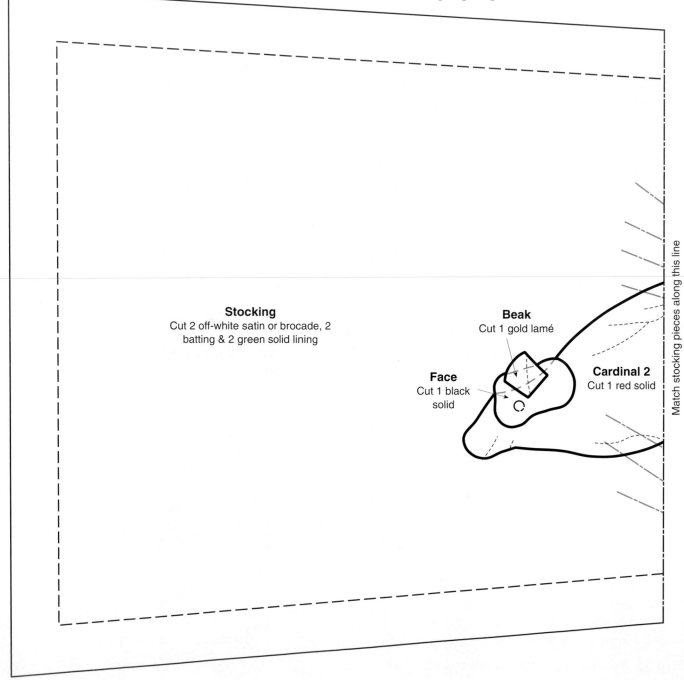

Stocking
Cut 2 off-white satin or brocade, 2
batting & 2 green solid lining

Beak
Cut 1 gold lamé

Face
Cut 1 black
solid

Cardinal 2
Cut 1 red solid

Match stocking pieces along this line

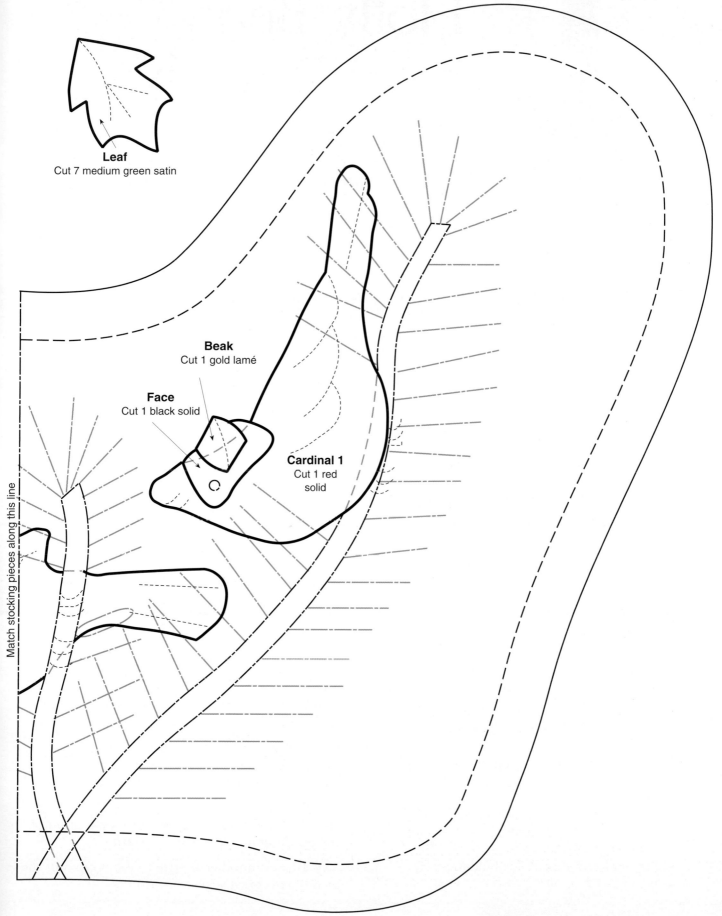

Leaf
Cut 7 medium green satin

Beak
Cut 1 gold lamé

Face
Cut 1 black solid

Cardinal 1
Cut 1 red
solid

Match stocking pieces along this line

Holly Berry Noel Wreath

By Eileen Westfall

No-sew appliqué is perfect for projects that are purely decorative and don't require washing.

No-Sew Appliqué

When you want a quick project for decorative purposes only, fusible web can be used to apply shapes to a background with no stitching needed. We used Quilter's Fusible Batting from June Tailor, Inc. to reduce the amount of quilting needed and create this project in an afternoon.

Project Specifications

Skill Level: Beginner
Quilt Size: 13" x 18"

Materials

- 9½" x 10½" rectangle white-on-white print for A
- 2 (2½" x 10½") strips dark green print for B
- 3 (2½" x 13½") strips green print for C
- 2 (2½" x 2½") squares red-and-cream check for D
- 2½" x 9½" strip white-on-white print for E
- 8" x 8" square tan check for inner and outer rings
- Scraps gold mottled, red-and-cream check, red solid, red print and light, dark and medium green prints
- Fat quarter red print for binding
- Backing 17" x 22"

- Quilter's Fusible Batting 17" x 22"
- Neutral color and white all-purpose thread
- ½ yard Steam-A-Seam 2 double-stick fusible web
- Basic sewing tools and supplies

Completing the Top

Step 1. Trace individual motifs onto the paper side of the fusible web. *Note: Patterns have already been reversed for tracing where necessary.*

Step 2. Cut out shapes, leaving a margin around each one.

Step 3. Fuse paper shapes to the wrong side of fabrics as directed on pattern for color. Cut out shapes on traced lines; remove paper backing.

Step 4. Fold and crease the A background piece to find the center.

Step 5. Center and arrange the wreath appliqué pieces on the A piece referring to the pattern for placement; fuse shapes in place, starting with the rings, then bows, leaves, candle, flame and berries, referring to the manufacturer's instructions.

Step 6. Referring to the Placement Diagram for Steps 6–10, sew B to opposite sides of A; press seams toward B.

Step 7. Sew C to the top and bottom of A; press seams toward C.

Step 8. Sew D to each short end of E; press seams toward E. Center and fuse the Noel message motif to the E strip referring to the pattern for positioning.

Step 9. Sew the fused D-E strip to the bottom of the pieced unit; press seams toward C.

Step 10. Sew another C strip to the bottom of the pieced unit; press seams toward C.

Finishing the Quilt

Step 1. Sandwich batting between the completed top and prepared backing piece; pin or baste layers together to hold flat for quilting.

Step 2. Quilt as desired by hand or machine. *Note: The quilt shown was machine-quilted in the ditch of A and E pieces using white all-purpose thread.*

Step 3. When quilting is complete, trim batting and backing even with quilted top; remove pins or basting.

Step 4. Cut two strips each 1¼" x 15" and 1¼" x 20" red print. Press under ¼" on one long edge of each strip.

Step 5. Center and sew a 1¼" x 20" strip to opposite sides of the sandwiched top matching raw edges of strip to raw edges of the quilt. Turn strips to the backside; hand-stitch in place. Trim excess at the ends.

Step 6. Repeat Step 5 on the quilt top and bottom; turn ends under even with quilt edge as shown in Figure 1; turn to the wrong side and hand-stitch in place to finish. ❖

Figure 1
Finish ends as shown.

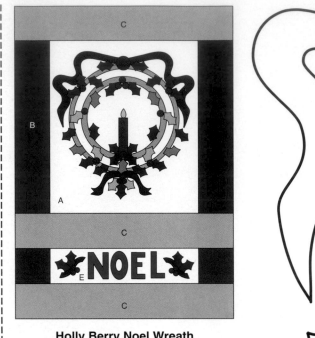

Match on dotted lines for full-size pattern

Holly Berry Noel Wreath
Placement Diagram
13" x 18"

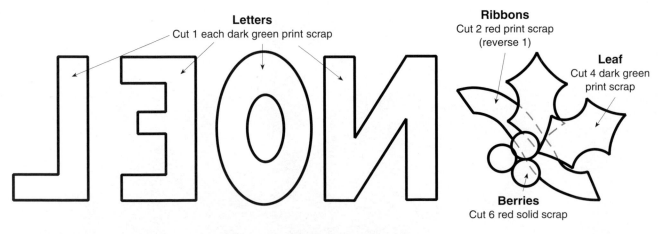

Letters
Cut 1 each dark green print scrap

Ribbons
Cut 2 red print scrap
(reverse 1)

Leaf
Cut 4 dark green
print scrap

Berries
Cut 6 red solid scrap

Message Motif

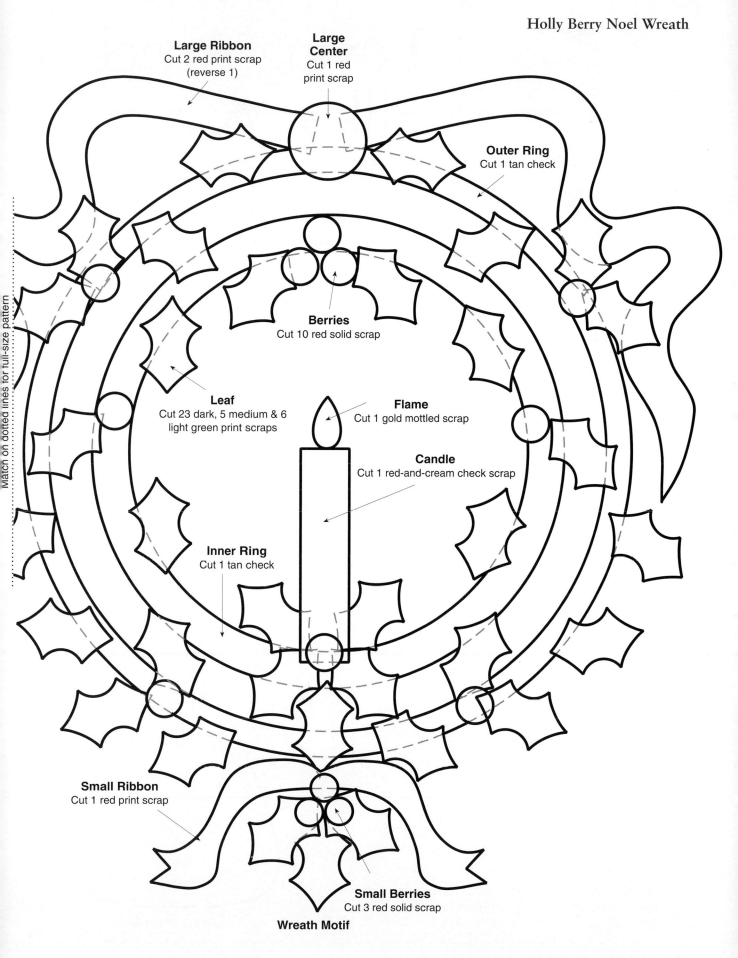

Large Ribbon
Cut 2 red print scrap
(reverse 1)

**Large
Center**
Cut 1 red
print scrap

Outer Ring
Cut 1 tan check

Berries
Cut 10 red solid scrap

Leaf
Cut 23 dark, 5 medium & 6
light green print scraps

Flame
Cut 1 gold mottled scrap

Candle
Cut 1 red-and-cream check scrap

Inner Ring
Cut 1 tan check

Match on dotted lines for full-size pattern

Small Ribbon
Cut 1 red print scrap

Small Berries
Cut 3 red solid scrap

Wreath Motif

Loving Angel Pillow & Card

By Chris Malone

Use chiffon to give a shadowed effect to the angel motif in the center of this pretty pillow and card combo.

Transparent Appliqué Technique

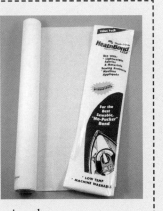

Iron-on adhesive web makes the transparent appliqué technique quicker and easier by holding the appliqué pieces firmly in place.

Project Specifications

Skill Level: Beginner
Pillow Size: 14" x 14" (without ruffle)
Card Size: 5" x 7"

Materials for Pillow

- ⅛ yard green print
- ⅓ yard ivory chiffon
- 1 yard Christmas print
- ⁷⁄₁₆" dark rose button
- 14" x 14" pillow form

Materials for Card

- 5" x 7" Christmas print
- 5" x 7" ivory chiffon
- 5" x 7" ivory card with 3½" x 5" opening
- Glue

Materials for Both

- Scraps blue tone-on-tone, ivory, dark rose and light and medium pink solids for appliqué
- All-purpose thread to match fabrics

- Blue, medium and dark rose, golden brown, dark brown and metallic gold 6-strand embroidery floss
- ¼ yard Therm O Web HeatnBond Lite Iron-On Adhesive
- Basic sewing tools and supplies

Making the Pillow

Step 1. Cut one 8½" x 8½" square each Christmas print and ivory chiffon.

Step 2. Trace angel pieces onto the paper side of the iron-on adhesive using the pattern given. Cut out shapes just outside traced lines.

Step 3. Referring to manufacturer's instructions, apply iron-on adhesive to the wrong side of the

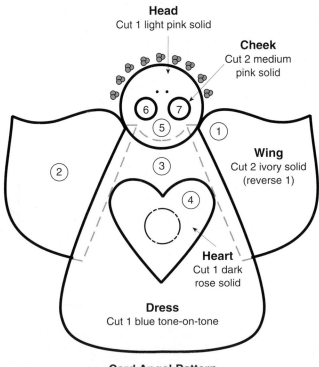

Head
Cut 1 light pink solid

Cheek
Cut 2 medium pink solid

Wing
Cut 2 ivory solid (reverse 1)

Heart
Cut 1 dark rose solid

Dress
Cut 1 blue tone-on-tone

Card Angel Pattern

fabric scraps as directed on the pattern for color and number to cut.

Step 4. Cut out shapes on traced lines; remove paper backing.

Step 5. Center the angel pieces in numerical order on the 8½" x 8½" fabric square cut in Step 1. When satisfied with placement, fuse in place.

Step 6. Pin the 8½" x 8½" square of ivory chiffon cut in Step 1 to the right side of the fused fabric square; machine-baste in place ⅛" from fabric edges.

Step 7. Use 1 strand of embroidery floss to sew a short running stitch around each section, using blue for the dress, metallic gold for the wings, medium rose for head and cheeks, and dark rose for the heart.

Step 8. Use 6 strands of golden brown embroidery floss to make French knots around top of head for hair as shown in Figure 1.

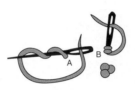

Step 9. Use 4 strands of dark brown embroidery floss to make two French knots for eyes.

Figure 1
Make French knots around top of head for hair.

Step 10. Sew the 7⁄16" dark rose button to the center of the heart with 2 strands dark rose embroidery floss.

Step 11. Cut two strips each 1" x 8½" (A) and 1" x 9½" (B) green print. Sew A to opposite sides and B to the top and bottom of the center angel square; carefully press seams toward strips.

Step 12. Cut two strips each 3" x 9½" (C) and 3" x 14½" (D) Christmas print. Sew C to opposite sides and D to the top and bottom of the pieced unit; carefully press seams toward strips.

Step 13. To make ruffle, cut three 5½" by fabric width strips Christmas print. Join on short ends to form a long tube.

Step 14. Fold the tube in half along length with wrong sides together to form a double-layered 2¾"-wide ruffle as shown in Figure 2.

Step 15. Sew two lines of gathering stitches ¼"

and ⅛" from raw edges of the folded tube as shown in Figure 3. Divide the tube into four equal sections and mark with a pin. Pull the stitches to gather and, with raw edges of ruffle and block together, pin a marked point to each corner. Adjust gathers evenly all around edges; pin and baste in place.

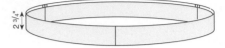

Figure 2
Fold the tube in half along length with wrong sides together to form a double-layered 2¾"-wide ruffle.

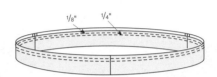

Figure 3
Sew 2 lines of gathering stitches ¼" and ⅛" from raw edges of the folded tube.

Sew 16. Cut two 9½" x 14½" rectangles Christmas print for pillow back. Fold and press under ¼" on one long edge of each rectangle; fold under ½" to make a double hem. Stitch in place.

Step 17. Place pillow front on a flat surface right side up. Pin ruffled edges down on each corner to prevent outer edges from getting caught in the seam.

Step 18. Lay one backing piece on top of the pillow front, right sides together with raw edges matching as shown in Figure 4 ; pin in place. Repeat with the second piece, overlapping the first piece 3", again referring to Figure 4. Stitch all around.

Figure 4
Lay 1 backing piece on top of the pillow front, right sides together with raw edges matching. Overlap pieces as shown.

Step 19. Turn right side out through opening on the backside; poke out corners and adjust ruffle. Insert the 14" x 14" pillow form through back opening to finish.

Making the Card

Step 1. Use Card Angel Pattern to fit the 3½" x 5" card opening.

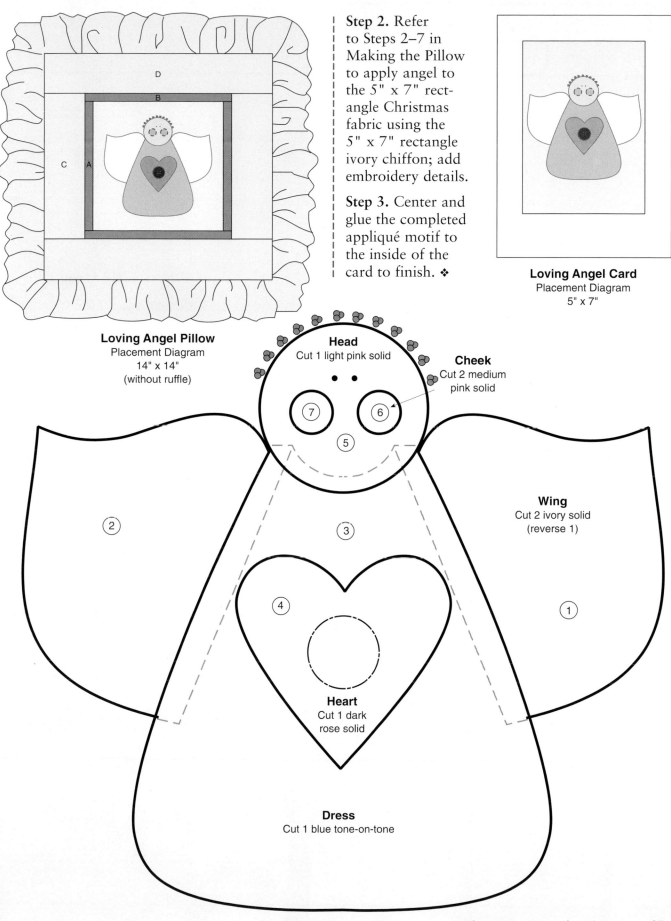

Step 2. Refer to Steps 2–7 in Making the Pillow to apply angel to the 5" x 7" rectangle Christmas fabric using the 5" x 7" rectangle ivory chiffon; add embroidery details.

Step 3. Center and glue the completed appliqué motif to the inside of the card to finish. ❖

Loving Angel Card
Placement Diagram
5" x 7"

Loving Angel Pillow
Placement Diagram
14" x 14"
(without ruffle)

Head
Cut 1 light pink solid

Cheek
Cut 2 medium pink solid

Wing
Cut 2 ivory solid
(reverse 1)

Heart
Cut 1 dark rose solid

Dress
Cut 1 blue tone-on-tone

Pillow Angel Pattern

Cozy Comforts

Dresden Cabins

By Julie Weaver

Reproduction prints with the look of the 1930s make this beautiful bed-size quilt.

Interfacing Appliqué

Lightweight interfacing was used to create a smooth edge on the outer edges of the flowers. Heat-resistant template material helps create a perfect circle for the flower centers. I chose to use a machine buttonhole-stitch to appliqué pieces in place.

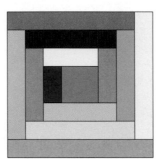

Log Cabin
8" x 8" Block

Dresden Cabin
15¼" x 15¼" Block

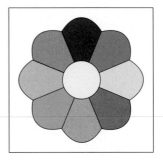

Dresden
10¾" x 10¾" Block

Project Specifications

Skill Level: Beginner

Quilt Size: 82½" x 97¾"

Block Size: 15¼" x 15¼", 10¾" x 10¾" and 8" x 8"

Number of Blocks: 20, 4 and 58

Materials

- ⅜ yard yellow print for flower centers
- 1 yard red print for binding
- 3 yards total reproduction prints for flower petals
- 4½ yards total reproduction prints for Log Cabins
- 4½ yards white solid
- Batting 89" x 104"
- Backing 89" x 104"
- Neutral color all-purpose thread
- Variegated machine-embroidery thread
- 3½ yards 22"-wide lightweight interfacing
- Heat-resistant template plastic
- Basic sewing tools and supplies

Making Blocks

Step 1. Cut 24 white solid 11¼" x 11¼" A squares for appliqué background. Fold and crease each square to mark centers. Set aside four A squares for corner blocks.

Step 2. Choose one reproduction print for Log Cabin block center B pieces. *Note: The quilt uses blue print for all B centers.* Cut four strips B fabric 2½" by fabric width; subcut into 2½" B squares. You will need 58 B squares.

Step 3. Cut 88 strips 1½" by fabric width reproduction prints for C.

Step 4. Sew B to a C strip as shown in Figure 1; trim edges of strip even with square and press seam toward C as shown in Figure 2.

Figure 1
Sew B to a C strip.

Figure 2
Trim edges of strip
even with square and
press seam toward C.

Step 5. Sew the B-C unit to a different C strip on the adjacent side as shown in Figure 3; trim edges of strip even with square and press seams toward C.

Figure 3
Sew the B-C unit to
a different C strip on
the adjacent side.

Step 6. Continue adding C strips around the B square until you have three C pieces on each side of B to complete one Log Cabin block as shown in Figure 4; repeat for 58 blocks.

Figure 4
Continue adding C strips around
the B square in numerical order
until you have 3 C pieces on each
side of B to complete 1 block.

Step 7. Cut each Log Cabin block in half on one diagonal as shown in Figure 5.

Figure 5
Cut each Log Cabin block
in half on 1 diagonal.

Step 8. Sew a Log Cabin triangle to each side of A referring to Figure 6; press seams toward A. Repeat for 20 A-B-C units.

Step 9. Trace the D petal pattern onto heat-resistant template plastic and cut out. Cut as directed on the pattern.

Figure 6
Sew a Log Cabin triangle
to each side of A.

Step 10. Arrange eight D pieces and join on straight seams to complete a D unit as shown in Figure 7; press seams in one direction. Repeat for 24 D units.

Figure 7
Arrange 8 D pieces and
join on straight seams
to complete a D unit.

Step 11. Cut twenty-four 10" x 10" squares lightweight interfacing.

Step 12. Layer one D unit right sides together with a square of lightweight interfacing; stitch all around outside edges. Trim seam and clip curves; turn right side out. Press to make smooth curves. Trim away lightweight interfacing to within ½"–1" of trimmed seam to reduce bulk.

Step 13. Trace flower center E piece onto heat-resistant template plastic; cut out. Cut as directed on pattern, adding 1½" all around.

Step 14. Run a gathering stitch about ¼" from outer edge of E; pull thread slightly and insert the template as shown in Figure 8. Pull gathering thread to form fabric shape around the template; press to sharpen edges. When template plastic has cooled, pop out the circle; press fabric circle flat again.

Figure 8
Run a gathering stitch about ¼"
from outer edge of E; pull thread
slightly and insert the template.

Step 15. Center and pin a D unit on an A-B-C unit using crease lines on A as a guide as shown in Figure 9.

Figure 9
Center and pin a D unit on an A-B-C unit using crease lines on A as a guide.

Step 16. Using variegated machine-embroidery thread in the top of the machine and all-purpose thread in the bobbin, machine buttonhole-stitch around the outer edges of the D unit.

Step 17. Center E on the stitched D unit and stitch in place as in Step 16 to complete one Dresden Cabin block; repeat for 20 blocks.

Step 18. Using the four remaining A squares, repeat Steps 15–17 to make four Dresden blocks for corners.

Completing the Top

Step 1. Arrange Dresden Cabin blocks in four rows of five blocks each. Join blocks in rows; press seams in one direction. Join rows to complete the pieced center; press seams in one direction.

Step 2. Cut and piece two 3⅝" x 76¾" F strips and two 3⅝" x 61½" G strips white solid; set aside.

Step 3. Cut five 16½" x 16½" H squares white solid; cut each square on both diagonals to make H triangles as shown in Figure 10.

Figure 10
Cut each H square on both diagonals to make H triangles.

Step 4. Sew a B-C unit to each short side of H as shown in Figure 11; press seams toward H.

Figure 11
Sew a B-C unit to each short side of H.

Dresden Cabins
Placement Diagram
82½" x 97¾"

Repeat for 18 B-C-H units.

Step 5. Join four B-C-H units to make a strip as shown in Figure 12; press seams in one direction. Repeat for two four-unit strips and two five-unit strips.

Figure 12
Join 4 B-C-H units to make a strip.

Step 6. Sew F to the H side of each five-unit strip as shown in Figure 13; press seams toward F. Repeat for two strips.

Figure 13
Sew F to the H side of each 5-unit strip.

Step 7. Sew a strip to opposite long sides of the pieced center referring to the Placement Diagram for positioning; press seams toward F.

Step 8. Sew G to the H side of each four-unit strip; press seams toward G.

Step 9. Sew a Dresden block to each end of the four-unit/G strips; press seams toward blocks.

Step 10. Sew a strip to the top and bottom of the pieced center; press seams toward strips.

Finishing the Quilt

Step 1. Sandwich batting between the completed top and prepared backing piece; pin or baste layers together to hold flat for quilting.

Step 2. Quilt as desired by hand or machine. *Note: The quilt shown was professionally machine-quilted using white thread.*

Step 3. When quilting is complete, trim batting and backing even with quilted top; remove pins or basting.

Step 4. Cut eleven 2¼" by fabric width strips red print; join strips on short ends to make one long strip for binding.

Step 5. Fold the binding strip in half along length with wrong sides together; press.

Step 6. Bind edges referring to the General Instructions. ❖

D
Cut 192 assorted
reproduction prints

E
Cut 24 yellow print

Add 1/2" seam allowance all around when cutting

Snow Star & Nine-Patch

By Jodi G. Warner

Even on a snowy night, the scribble-stitched snow stars on this lap quilt can keep you warm!

Scribble-Stitch Machine Appliqué

This technique offers a fun and creative way to add surface texture to the edges of fused appliqué shapes. Keep your sewing machine set for straight stitching, then drop the feed dogs, attach a spring darning foot and get ready for some free-motion fun.

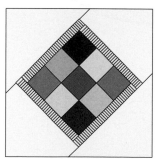

Nine-Patch Variation
9" x 9" Block

Snow Star
9" x 9" Block

Scribble-Stitch Machine Appliqué

Supplies & Equipment
- Appliqué and background fabrics
- Appliqué design or test-shape templates
- 5mm mechanical or other sharp pencil

- Lightweight fusible web
- Sewing machine with spring darning foot attached
- Fabric and paper scissors
- Thread to match appliqué fabrics
- Small spring embroidery hoop (optional)

Instructions

Step 1. Trace appliqué shapes onto the paper side of the fusible web. Turn non-symmetrical shapes over and trace to make reverse images so they will appear correct from the fabric front.

Step 2. Cut out shapes, leaving a margin around each one.

Step 3. Fuse each shape to the wrong side of the appropriate fabrics referring to the manufacturer's instructions, considering grain lines or fabric patterns as shapes are positioned before applying heat.

Step 4. Carefully trim each shape on traced lines; remove paper backing.

Step 5. Position shapes on the right side of the selected background fabric according to design layout, overlapping edges as required. When satisfied with placement, fuse shapes in place.

Step 6. Determine the best order for completing the scribble stitching; stitch first around shapes that are overlapped by other edges.

Step 7. Thread the machine top and bobbin with a thread color coordinated to the first appliqué piece; drop the feed dogs and attach a spring darning foot. If desired, center the background fabric in an inverted spring hoop to help stabilize it during stitching.

Step 8. Select a stitching pattern. Many variations are possible, including a variable zigzag, continuous loops or feather stitches. Insert the needle through the work and draw the bobbin thread to the top to help avoid tangling on the backside. Hold the threads out of the way, take a few stitches in place to lock, then begin free-motion stitching along the edge of the appliqué. Scribble stitching should barely overlap the raw edge and extend into the appliqué piece approximately ¼".

Step 9. When approaching the end of one stitching run, take a few stitches in place to lock, then raise the presser foot and remove the work from the machine. Trim thread ends neatly or pull them to the backside. Complete scribble stitching in sequence for remaining edges, changing thread color as needed.

Snow Star & Nine-Patch Lap Quilt

Project Specifications
  Skill Level: Beginner
  Quilt Size: 53¼" x 63½"
  Block Size: 9" x 9"
  Number of Blocks: 20

Materials
- 5 blue and 4 pink 2" x 20" B scrap strips for Nine-Patch blocks
- ¼ yard pink-with-blue print for F
- ⅝ yard white-on-white print for snow stars
- ⅝ yard cream print for D
- ¾ yard cream/navy stripe for C and binding
- 1 yard dark blue mottled for E
- 1 yard medium blue print for A
- 1⅝ yards cream print for borders
- Batting 60" x 70"

- Backing 60" x 70"
- Neutral color all-purpose thread
- Silver metallic thread
- Blue and cream quilting thread
- 1¼ yards medium-to-heavyweight fusible web
- ⅛" paper punch
- Basic sewing tools and supplies and spring darning foot

Making Snow Star Blocks

Step 1. Cut ten 10" x 10" A squares medium blue print; fold and crease squares to mark centers. *Note: The A squares are cut ½" larger than needed to adjust for potential shrinking from machine-appliqué. Squares are trimmed after stitching is complete.*

Step 2. Prepare template for snow star shape using pattern given. Trace the shape on the paper side of the fusible web referring to pattern for number to cut.

Step 3. Cut out shapes, leaving a margin around each one. Fuse onto the wrong side of the white-on-white print. Cut out shapes on traced lines.

Step 4. Use the ⅛" paper punch to cut out circles where indicated on pattern; remove paper backing.

Step 5. Position a snow star shape on the right side of one A square, aligning a pair of large outer points with vertical creases in A and the inner points with the horizontal creases in A referring to Figure 1; fuse in place. Repeat for 10 blocks.

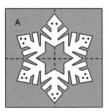

Figure 1
Align a pair of large outer points with vertical creases in A and the inner points with the horizontal creases in A.

Step 6. Complete scribble stitching to secure all raw edges in place using silver metallic thread in the top of the machine and all-purpose thread in the bobbin and referring to the close-up photo of one block. *Note: To make stitching continuous, stitch up to the outer point, down across punched*

areas, then return to point and continue. Excess fusible on the machine needle can be wiped away regularly with rubbing alcohol.

Step 7. Trim stitched squares to 9½" x 9½", keeping snow stars centered on A to complete Snow Star blocks.

Making Nine-Patch Blocks

Step 1. Join one pink and two blue B strips right sides together along length to make a B1 strip set; press seams in one direction. Repeat for two B1 strip sets. Join one blue and two pink B strips to make a B2 strip set; press seams in one direction. Subcut strip sets into 2" segments. You will need 10 segments from each strip set.

Step 2. Join one B2 segment and one B1 segment from each strip set to complete a B unit as shown in Figure 2; press seams in one direction. Repeat for 10 B units.

Figure 2
Join B segments to complete a B unit.

Step 3. Cut one 5½" by fabric width C strip cream/navy stripe; subcut strip into 1" C segments.

Step 4. Sew one C to one side of B, stopping stitching 1" from end of C as shown in Figure 3.

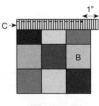

Figure 3
Sew C to 1 side of B, stopping stitching 1" from end of C.

Step 5. Fold the attached C strip back; press seam toward C. Stitch a second C strip to the attached C end of the B-C unit as shown in Figure 4; press seam toward C. Add a strip to the two remaining sides of B, holding the first C strip out of the way when stitching the last strip as shown in Figure 5; press seam toward C.

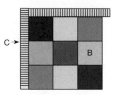

Figure 4
Stitch a second C strip to the
attached C end of the B-C unit.

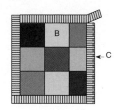

Figure 5
Hold the first C strip out
of the way when stitching
the last C strip.

Step 6. Reposition the first C strip and complete seam stitching as shown in Figure 6; press.

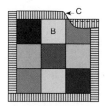

Figure 6
Reposition the first C strip and
complete seam stitching.

Figure 7
Cut each D square
on 1 diagonal to
make D triangles.

Step 7. Cut twenty 6" x 6" squares cream print for D; cut each D square on one diagonal as shown in Figure 7 to make D triangles.

Step 8. Fold and crease each D triangle to find the center as shown in Figure 8.

Figure 8
Fold and crease each D
triangle to find the center.

Step 9. Sew D to opposite sides of a B-C unit, matching center crease with center of the B-C unit; stitch. Press seams toward D; trim excess triangle tails even with C as shown in Figure 9.

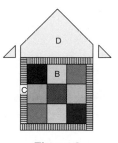

Figure 9
Trim excess triangle
tails even with C.

Step 10. Sew D to the remaining opposite sides of the B-C-D unit, matching center crease with center of the B-C unit. Press seams toward D to complete one Nine-Patch Variation block. Repeat for ten blocks.

Completing the Top

Step 1. Cut three 9½" by fabric width strips dark

blue mottled; subcut strips into 1¾" E segments. You will need 49 E segments.

Step 2. Cut two 1¾" by fabric width strips pink-with-blue print for F; subcut strips into thirty 1¾" x 1¾" F squares.

Step 3. Join five F and four E pieces to make a sashing strip as shown in Figure 10; repeat for six sashing strips. Press seams toward F.

Figure 10
Join 5 F and 4 E pieces
to make a sashing strip.

Step 4. Join five E pieces with Nine-Patch Variation and Snow Star blocks to make a block row as shown in Figure 11; repeat for five block rows. Press seams toward E.

Figure 11
Join 5 E pieces with Nine-Patch
Variation and Snow Star blocks to
make block rows.

Step 5. Arrange the sashing rows with the block rows referring to the Placement Diagram for positioning of the block rows. Join in rows; join rows to complete the pieced center. Press seams toward the sashing rows.

Step 6. Cut two 6" x 53" G strips and two 6" x 53¾" H strips along length of cream print. Sew a G strip to opposite long sides and H strips to the top and bottom of the pieced center; press seams toward strips.

Finishing the Quilt

Step 1. Sandwich batting between the completed top and prepared backing piece; pin or baste layers together to hold flat for quilting.

Step 2. Quilt as desired by hand or machine. *Note: The quilt shown was machine-quilted in the D pieces using the pattern given and blue quilting thread and in ¼" echo lines outside C strips and ½" echo lines around the snow star shape and in a purchased braided cable pattern in the G and H border strips using white quilting thread.*

Step 3. When quilting is complete, trim batting

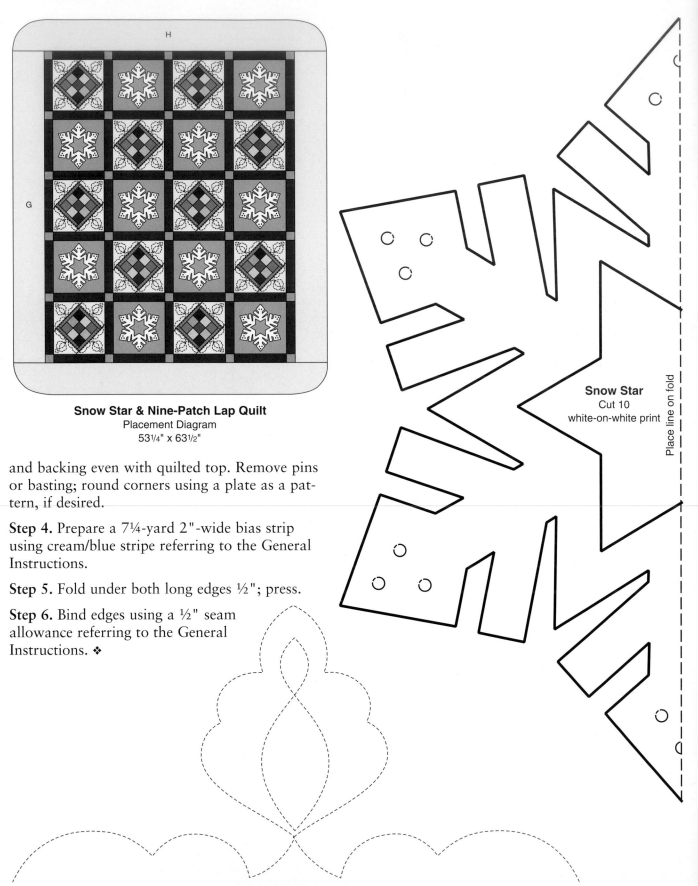

Snow Star & Nine-Patch Lap Quilt
Placement Diagram
53¼" x 63½"

and backing even with quilted top. Remove pins or basting; round corners using a plate as a pattern, if desired.

Step 4. Prepare a 7¼-yard 2"-wide bias strip using cream/blue stripe referring to the General Instructions.

Step 5. Fold under both long edges ½"; press.

Step 6. Bind edges using a ½" seam allowance referring to the General Instructions. ❖

Snow Star
Cut 10
white-on-white print

Place line on fold

Quilting Design for D

Counting Sheep

By Judith Sandstrom

If you have trouble sleeping, why not count the sheep on your quilt? Look for the one and only black sheep in the group.

Light-on-Dark Appliqué

Use a medium-weight fusible interfacing on the wrong side of light fabrics to prevent shadowing of darker fabrics underneath.

Sheep
12" x 12" Block

Project Specifications

Skill Level: Beginner
Quilt Size: 81½" x 98"
Block Size: 12" x 12"
Number of Blocks: 20

Materials

- ¼ yard black mottled
- ⅓ yard rose tone-on-tone
- ½ yard tan tone-on-tone
- 1⅛ yards white-on-white print
- 1⅝ yards floral for borders
- 2½ yards white/blue sky print
- 3¼ yards green-on-green print
- Batting 88" x 104"
- Backing 88" x 104"
- Neutral color all-purpose thread
- Black, cream, rose and tan machine-embroidery thread
- Quilting thread
- 1 yard medium-weight fusible interfacing
- 3 yards Pellon Wonder-Under fusible web
- 3½ yards Stitch-n-Tear fabric stabilizer
- Basic sewing tools and supplies

Making Sheep Blocks

Step 1. Cut twenty 12½" x 12½" A squares green-on-green print; fold and crease to mark centers.

Step 2. Apply medium-weight fusible interfacing to the wrong side of ½ yard white-on-white print.

Step 3. Prepare templates for sheep pieces; trace the sheep pattern pieces on the paper side of the fusible web as directed on patterns for number to cut. Cut out shapes, leaving a margin around each one. *Note: The patterns are already reversed.*

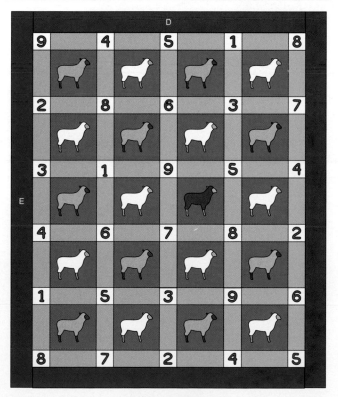

Counting Sheep
Placement Diagram
81½" x 98"

Step 4. Fuse shapes to the wrong side of the fabrics as directed on each piece for color, using the interfaced section for the white-on-white print sheep. Cut out shapes on traced lines; remove paper backing.

Step 5. Center a sheep motif on A, layering in numerical order; fuse in place. Repeat for 20 blocks.

Step 6. Cut twenty 10" x 10" squares fabric stabilizer; pin a square behind each fused A square.

Step 7. Using machine-embroidery thread to match fabrics, machine zigzag-stitch around each shape. When stitching is complete, remove fabric stabilizer.

Making Letter Blocks

Step 1. Bond fusible web to the wrong side of the rose tone-on-tone.

Step 2. Prepare letter patterns using pattern pieces given; trace shapes onto the fused paper side of the rose tone-on-tone as directed for each number.

Step 3. Cut out shapes on traced lines; remove paper backing.

Step 4. Cut four 5" by fabric width strips white-on-white print; subcut into 5" square segments for B; you will need 30 B squares. Fold each square and crease to mark centers.

Step 5. Center a number on each square; fuse in place.

Step 6. Cut 30 squares fabric stabilizer 4" x 4"; pin a square to the wrong side of each fused B square. Using rose machine-embroidery thread in the top of the machine and all-purpose thread in the bobbin, machine zigzag-stitch around number shapes. When stitching is complete, remove fabric stabilizer.

Completing the Top

Step 1. Cut seven strips white/blue sky print 12½" by fabric width for C; subcut strips into 5" rectangle segments for C. You will need 49 C rectangles.

Step 2. Join four Sheep blocks with five C pieces to make a block row as shown in Figure 1; repeat for five rows referring to the Placement Diagram for positioning of sheep in the rows. Press seams toward C.

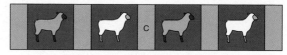

Figure 1
Join 4 sheep blocks with 5 C pieces to make a block row.

Step 3. Arrange five number squares and four C pieces to make a sashing row referring to the Placement Diagram and Figure 2; repeat for six rows. Join in rows; press seams toward C. *Note: There is no special order for the numbers. They can be placed in random positions or in numerical order as desired.*

Figure 2
Join 5 number squares with 4 C pieces to make a sashing row.

Step 4. Join the sashing rows with the block rows, beginning and ending with a sashing row; press seams toward sashing rows.

Step 5. Cut and piece two 6" x 71" D strips and two 6" x 98½" E strips floral. Sew a D strip to the top and bottom and the E strips to opposite long sides of the pieced center; press seams toward strips.

Finishing the Quilt

Step 1. Sandwich batting between the completed top and prepared backing piece; pin or baste layers together to hold flat for quilting.

Step 2. Quilt as desired by hand or machine. *Note: The quilt shown was hand-quilted ¼" from seams using tan quilting thread.*

Step 3. When quilting is complete, trim batting and backing even with quilted top; remove pins or basting.

Step 4. Cut nine 2¼" by fabric width strips green-on-green print; join strips on short ends to make one long strip for binding.

Step 5. Fold the binding strip in half along length with wrong sides together; press.

Step 6. Bind edges referring to the General Instructions. ❖

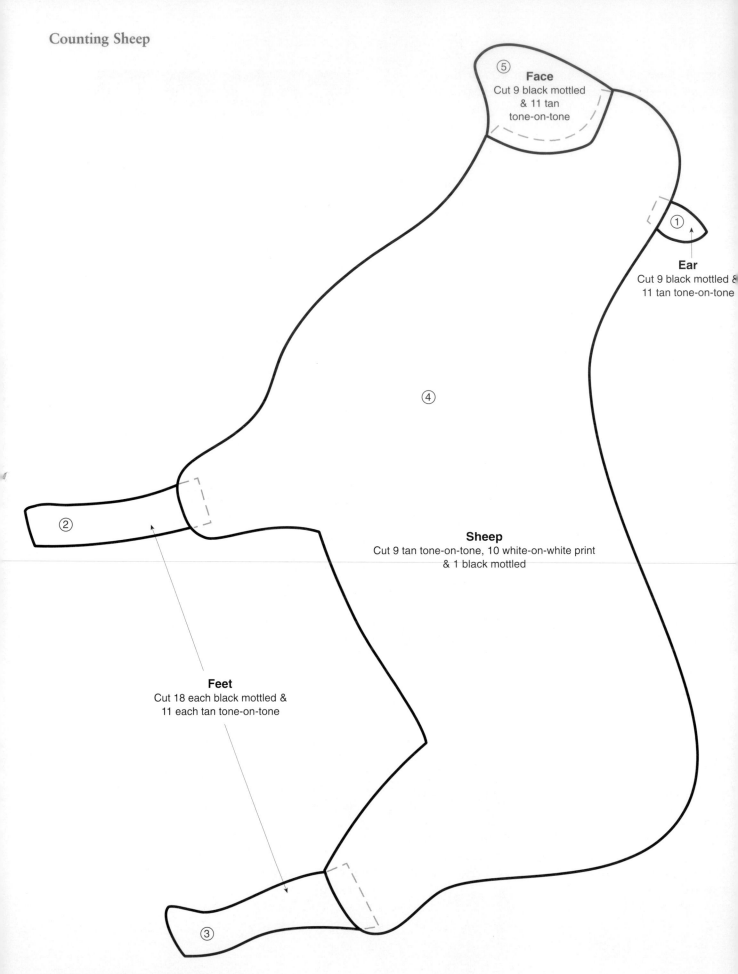

Face
Cut 9 black mottled
& 11 tan
tone-on-tone

Ear
Cut 9 black mottled &
11 tan tone-on-tone

Sheep
Cut 9 tan tone-on-tone, 10 white-on-white print
& 1 black mottled

Feet
Cut 18 each black mottled &
11 each tan tone-on-tone

Numbers
Cut 3 each 1, 2, 3 & 7, 4 each 4, 5 & 8, and 6 number 6 rose tone-on-tone
Note: Use the number 6 upside down for number 9

All That Jazz

By Patsy S. Moreland

Liven up a room with this music-theme wall quilt and wall strips.

Glue Appliqué

Use crafter's glue to adhere buttons and other embellishments to this wall quilt.

Wall Quilt

Project Specifications
Skill Level: Beginner
Quilt Size: 20½" x 28"

Materials
- Scraps orange mottled and bright yellow, gold and tan tone-on tones
- 10" x 10" square 1" black-and-white check
- 6" x 6" square ¾" black-and-white check
- ⅛ yard each gold and turquoise lamés
- ⅛ yard blue mottled
- ⅓ yard black-with-silver stars
- ⅓ yard white-with-black dot
- ⅓ yard black-with-white dot
- ½ yard white-on-white print
- ⅔ yard music print
- Fusible fleece 26" x 34"
- All-purpose thread to match fabrics
- ½ yard Steam-A-Seam 2 double stick fusible web

- 1 spool Clover No. 700 BGY fusible bias tape
- 1 package Scrapbooking Music die cuts Westrim Crafts No. 28009 PE101
- 1 package each Blumenthal Lansing Primary Favorite Things buttons No. 442 and High Five No. 32 hand buttons
- 1 skein black DMC pearl cotton
- Crafter's Pick Ultimate Glue
- 1 Putting on the Glitz Jewel Box Kit by Westrim No. 4879
- 1 package 1" bone rings
- Press cloth and No. 20 large-eye needle
- Basic sewing tools and supplies

Completing the Top

Step 1. Cut three 6½" x 6½" squares each music print (A) and black-with-silver stars (B).

Step 2. Cut one 6½" by fabric width strip white-with-black dot; subcut strip into seven 2" segments for C.

Step 3. Cut two 2" x 2" squares ¾" black-and-white check for D as shown in Figure 1.

Figure 1
Cut two 2" x 2"
squares ¾"
black-and-white
check for D.

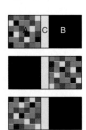

Figure 2
Join 1 each A and B squares
with C to make a row.

Step 4. Join one each A and B squares with C to make a row; repeat for three rows referring to Figure 2 for positioning of pieces. ***Note:*** *If your A squares have a definite one-way, upright design, be sure to sew them in this position.* Press seams toward C.

Step 5. Join two C pieces with D to make a C-D row as shown in Figure 3; repeat for two rows. Press seams toward C.

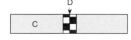

Figure 3
Join 2 C pieces with D
to make a C-D row.

Step 6. Cut four 2½" x 2½" squares 1" black-and-white check for E as for D.

Step 7. Cut two 2½" x 14" F strips and two 2½" x 21½" G strips white-on-white print.

Step 8. Sew G to opposite long sides of the pieced center; press seams toward G. Sew E to each end of each F strip; sew to the top and bottom of the pieced center. Press seams toward strips.

Step 9. Cut two 2" x 21" H strips and two 2" x 25½" J strips music print. Sew J strips to opposite long sides and H strips to the top and bottom of the pieced center; press seams toward strips.

Step 10. Bond the fusible fleece to the wrong side of the pieced top referring to manufacturer's instructions.

Step 11. Trim fusible fleece piece to the same size as the pieced top; cut a backing piece this same size.

Step 12. Place the backing wrong sides together with the pieced top/fleece layers; press to bond layers together.

Step 13. Using black pearl cotton, tie square knots through the center of each A, B, C and D piece referring to Figure 4.

Figure 4
Make a square knot as shown.

Step 14. Cut three 2¼" by fabric width strips black-with-white dot; join strips on short ends to make one long strip for binding.

Step 15. Fold the binding strip in half along length with wrong sides together; press.

Step 16. Bind edges referring to the General Instructions.

Quilt Embellishments

Step 1. Trace die-cut shapes onto one paper side of the fusible web as follows: two gold lamé and two turquoise lamé notes (one reversed); four tan scrap stars, one bright yellow saxophone, one gold trumpet and two each small and large blue mottled scrolls. Cut out shapes leaving a margin around each one. Remove paper liner and bond to the wrong side of fabrics as directed above for color; cut out shapes on traced lines. Remove remaining paper backing.

Step 2. Arrange the shapes on the completed quilt top referring to the Placement Diagram for positioning; fuse in place, using a press cloth to protect the lamé shapes.

All That Jazz
Placement Diagram
20½" x 28"

Step 3. Cut one 13" and two 8½" lengths fusible bias tape; angle each end of each length as shown in Figure 5. Center one 8½" length at the bottom of each G strip and the 13" length in the center of the bottom F strip referring to the Placement Diagram.

Figure 5
Angle ends of
fusible bias tape.

Step 4. Arrange and glue one each orange, yellow, blue and green ¼" buttons above the bias strip on the G strips. Glue one large glitz star to the center of the top F strip. Remove thread loop on the back of the hand buttons with scissors; glue one hand button on each side of the glitz star.

Step 5. Glue glitz jewels in random placement on A squares and in the center of each D and E square.

Step 6. Evenly space and hand-stitch the 1" bone rings 2" from top backside edge for hanging to finish.

Companion Wall Pieces

Leftover fabrics and findings from the wall quilt are used to create stick-on companion wall pieces. Additional materials needed are listed below.

Project Specifications
Size: 20" x 5¼"

Materials
- Pres-On Self Stick 30 pt. white plastic board high tack
- 1 package Pres-On Goosh 1" mounting squares
- 1 package ¼" Therm O Web Peel n Stick doubled sided adhesive

Instructions

Step 1. Cut two 1½" by fabric width strips white-with-black dot and one 1½" by fabric width strip black-with-silver stars.

Step 2. Sew the black-with-silver stars strip between the two white-with-black dot strips to make a strip set; press seams toward darker fabric.

Step 3. Subcut strip set into six 3½" S segments as shown in Figure 6.

Figure 6
Subcut strip set into
3½" S segments.

Step 4. Cut four 3½" x 6½" T rectangles music print.

Step 5. Join three S segments and two T rectangles to make an S-T strip as shown in Figure 7; repeat for two strips. Press seams toward T.

Figure 7
Join 3 S segments and 2 T
rectangles to make an S-T strip.

Step 6. Cut four 2½" x 21½" V strips white-on-white print. Sew a strip to opposite long sides of each pieced strip referring to Figure 8.

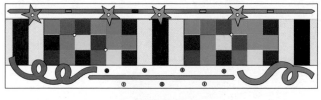

Jazz Wall Piece
Placement Diagram
20" x 5¼"

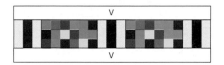

Figure 8
Sew a V strip to opposite long
sides of each pieced strip.

Step 7. Cut four each 6" and 20" pieces double-sided adhesive. Remove paper from one side of each strip; stick to the wrong-side edges of each pieced strip.

Step 8. Cut two pieces white plastic board 5¼" x 20". Peel away the red printed paper back. Center a fabric motif strip on the board and press on the sticky side of the board. Repeat for both strips. Peel paper off double-sided adhesive on fabrics and stick edges down on the backside of the plastic board.

Step 9. Prepare star and scroll shapes as in Step 1 for Quilt Embellishments, cutting eight tan scrap stars and two each small and large blue mottled scrolls. Arrange on each strip referring to the Placement Diagram; fuse in place.

Step 10. Cut two 11" and two 20" lengths fusible bias; angle ends. Center and fuse one long strip to the top of each strip and a shorter strip to the bottom.

Step 11. Glue a total of seven ¼" buttons (1 each red, green and blue and two each orange and yellow) above and below each 11" fused bias strip referring to the Placement Diagram for positioning.

Step 12. Glue a glitz jewel in the center of each star and along the 20" fused bias strip between stars and randomly on the T rectangles to finish the wall strips.

Step 13. Mount on the wall with six 1" mounting squares per strip. ❖

Fall Fantasy

By Connie Rand

Use leaves from your own yard or a nearby park, or collect some while you're on vacation to make this colorful quilt. Leaf shapes can be overlapped or placed in a circle. Try combining different shapes in some of the blocks.

Finding Appliqué Patterns in Nature

Appliqué patterns can come from many sources. For something a little different, look around outside for some inspiration. Leaves are everywhere, and come in many shapes and sizes. Oak and maple leaves have wonderful complicated shapes, and compound leaves can be taken apart to provide simpler shapes. Use your imagination and raid your scrap collection for a really unique quilt.

Project Specifications

Skill Level: Intermediate
Quilt Size: 66" x 81"
Block Size: 12" x 12"
Number of Blocks: 12

Materials

- Assorted bright-colored scraps for leaves
- Scrap fabrics totaling 4 yards or 15 fat quarters for A, B, C and D
- Twelve 12½" x 12½" squares assorted light prints for leaf block backgrounds
- ½ yard dark blue print for B and E
- ⅝ yard light blue print for binding
- Batting 72" x 85"
- Backing 72" x 85"
- Neutral color all-purpose thread
- Gold metallic thread
- 4 yards HeatnBond fusible web (amount varies based on leaves used)
- Basic sewing tools and supplies and water-erasable marker or pencil

Completing the Top

Step 1. Cut 31 strips 3½" x 12½" for A, 74 squares 3½" x 3½" for B and 82 strips 3½" x 6½" for D from scraps or fat quarters.

Step 2. From dark blue print, cut 24 squares 3½" x 3½" for B and four squares 6½" x 6½" for C.

Step 3. Use leaf patterns provided, or find your own leaves and trace on paper side of fusible web. Cut out each shape, leaving a margin around each one.

Step 4. Fuse leaf shapes to the wrong side of assorted bright-colored scraps; cut out shapes on traced lines. Remove paper backing and arrange on light print squares as desired, referring to the Placement Diagram for suggestions; fuse in place.

Step 5. Satin-stitch around leaves using gold metallic thread in the top of the machine and all-purpose thread in the bobbin.

Step 6. Join three leaf blocks with four A strips to make a row as shown in Figure 1; repeat for four rows.

Figure 1
Join 3 blocks with 4 A strips
to make a row.

Step 7. Join four B squares with three A strips to make a sashing row as shown in Figure 2; repeat for five rows.

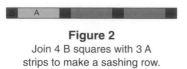

Figure 2
Join 4 B squares with 3 A
strips to make a sashing row.

Step 8. Join leaf rows with sashing rows as shown in Figure 3; press seams toward sashing rows.

Figure 3
Join leaf rows and
sashing rows as shown.

Figure 4
Join B and C squares as
shown; sew to pieced center.

Step 9. Join 21 C squares to make a strip; repeat for two strips. Sew strips to opposite long sides of the pieced center as shown in Figure 4.

Step 10. Join 16 C squares to make a strip; add a B square to each end. Repeat for two strips. Sew a strip to the top and bottom of pieced center, again referring to Figure 4.

Step 11. Join 23 D strips on long sides to make a border strip; repeat for two border strips. Sew a strip to opposite sides of pieced center as shown in Figure 5.

Figure 5
Join D strips and sew to
opposite sides as shown.

Step 12. Join 18 D strips on long sides to make a border strip; repeat for two border strips. Sew an E square to each end of each border strip as shown in Figure 6. Sew a strip to the top and bottom of the pieced center to complete the top.

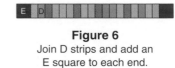

Figure 6
Join D strips and add an
E square to each end.

Finishing the Quilt

Step 1. Sandwich batting between the completed top and prepared backing piece; pin or baste layers together to hold flat for quilting.

Step 2. Quilt as desired by hand or machine. *Note: The quilt shown was professionally machine-quilted using variegated thread.*

Step 3. When quilting is complete, trim batting and batting even with quilted top; remove pins or basting.

Step 4. Cut eight 2¼" by fabric width strips light blue print.

Fall Fantasy
Placement Diagram
66" x 81"

Step 5. Fold the binding strip in half along length with wrong sides together; press.

Step 6. Bind edges referring to the General Instructions. ❖

Leaf Patterns
Cut scraps as desired

Fall Fantasy

Leaf Patterns
Cut scraps as desired

Nodding Tulips

By Ruth Swasey

The bright-colored tulip appliqués are highlighted by strip-pieced border triangles in shades of green in this fabric garden.

Tulip
8" x 8" Block

Project Specifications

Skill Level: Beginner
Quilt Size: Approximately 82" x 87"
Block Size: 8" x 8"
Number of Blocks: 50

Materials

- ½ yard each light (#1), medium (#2) and dark (#5) green prints or tone-on-tones for pieced triangles
- ¾ yard lime-green tone-on-tone for borders and pieced triangles (#4)
- ¾ yard total of a variety of prints and tone-on-tones in flower colors for tulips
- 1½ yards green print for borders and pieced triangles (#3)
- 2 yards green mottled for leaves and stems
- 2¼ yards green Bali print for sashing and binding
- 2½ yards white-on-white print for block background
- Batting 88 x 93"
- Backing 88" x 93"
- All-purpose thread to match fabrics
- White machine-quilting thread
- 1¾ yards lightweight fabric stabilizer
- Heat-resistant template material
- Spray starch
- Small paintbrush
- Basic sewing tools and supplies

Making Tulip Blocks

Step 1. Cut 10 white-on-white print strips 8½" by fabric width; subcut strips into 8½" square segments for A. You will need 50 A squares for appliqué background. Fold and crease each square on both diagonals.

Step 2. Prepare heat-resistant templates for appliqué shapes using patterns given. Cut fabric shapes as directed, adding a ¼" seam allowance all around when cutting.

Step 3. Spray some spray starch into the can's cover.

Step 4. To prepare appliqué shapes, select one fabric shape and its matching heat-resistant template. Center the template on the wrong side of the fabric shape; using the small paintbrush, paint a small amount of spray starch on the seam allowance of the fabric patch. Press the edges of the fabric

patch over the template; remove the template. Repeat for all appliqué shapes. *Note: This method gives a crisp, smooth edge for the machine-stitching step.*

Step 5. Center a stem piece at one diagonal corner of A as shown in Figure 1; slip one leaf shape under stem and pin in place referring to full-size motif for positioning. Place a tulip shape at the tip of the stem.

Figure 1
Center the stem at 1 diagonal corner.

Step 6. Using all-purpose thread to match fabrics, straight-stitch close to the edge of each shape to secure pieces to A. Repeat for 50 blocks. *Note: It saves time if you stitch all leaf and stem pieces using the same color thread and then all tulip shapes of the same color at one time. This saves time in repeated thread changes.*

Making Strip-Pieced Triangles

Step 1. Cut and piece two strips lime green tone-on-tone (#4) 2½" x 82⅛" for L; set aside for borders.

Step 2. Cut fabric-width strips as follows from green fabrics #1–#5: five 2½" strips and one 1¾" strip fabric #1; four 2¼" strips and one 1¾" strip fabric #2; eight 2" strips fabric #3; six 1¼" strips and one 1½" strip fabric #4; and four 2½" strips fabric #5.

Step 3. Cut nine 10⅜" x 10⅜" squares lightweight fabric stabilizer.

Step 4. Place a 2½" #1 strip on one stabilizer square from corner to corner as shown in Figure 2; trim excess length. Sew a 1¼" #4 strip to each side of the center, placing the #4 strips right sides together with #1. Press #2 strips to the right side; trim excess length. Press after each strip is stitched. Continue adding strips on each side of the center until the stabilizer is covered as shown in Figure 3. Repeat to cover all stabilizer squares.

Figure 2
Center and pin a 2½" #1 strip to 1 stabilizer square from corner to corner.

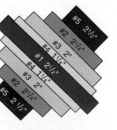

Figure 3
Continue adding strips on each side of the center in numerical fabric order until the stabilizer is covered.

Step 5. Trim excess fabric strips even with stabilizer squares as shown in Figure 4.

Figure 4
Trim excess fabric strips even with stabilizer square.

Figure 5
Cut down the center from 1 diagonal corner to the other, cutting through the center of the #1 strip to make 2 B triangles.

Step 6. Cut down the center from one diagonal corner to the other, cutting through the center of the #1 strip to make two B triangles as shown in Figure 5. Repeat to complete 18 B triangles.

Step 7. Cut two 8⅝" x 8⅝" squares lightweight fabric stabilizer. Draw a line 1" from edge all around each square as shown in Figure 6.

Figure 6
Draw a line 1" from edge all around square.

Figure 7
Trim strip so ends just touch line.

Step 8. Place a 2½" #5 strip from corner to corner along one diagonal of a stabilizer square; trim excess length to leave ends of strip just touching the drawn lines as shown in Figure 7.

Step 9. Cover remaining area within the drawn lines referring to Figure 8 for fabric order and strip widths.

Figure 8
Cover remaining area within drawn lines.

Figure 9
Align edge of strip with drawn line; trim ends even with lines on adjacent sides. Stitch ¼" from edge.

Step 10. Place a #3 strip on opposite sides of the stitched square, aligning edge of strip with the drawn line; pin in place. Trim excess at ends even with lines on adjacent sides as shown in Figure 9.

Stitch ¼" from edge; press strips to the right side. Sew #3 strips to the remaining sides; press to the right side. Trim pieced square edges with stabilizer square.

Step 11. Cut along the diagonal center to make two C triangles as shown in Figure 10. Repeat with second square to make four C triangles.

Figure 10
Cut along diagonal center to make 2 C triangles.

Completing the Top

Step 1. Cut three strips green Bali print 8½" by fabric width; subcut strips into 2" segments to make D sashing strips. Repeat for 60 D sashing strips.

Step 2. Lay out blocks in diagonal rows with D strips as shown in Figure 11; join in diagonal rows. Press seams toward D.

Step 3. Cut fifteen 2" strips green Bali print; join on short ends and trim to make two strips each 11½" for E, 30½" for F, 49½" for G, 68½" for H, 87½" for I and one strip 97" for J.

Step 4. Arrange the strips with the sashed block rows and the B and C triangles as shown in Figure 12 and stitch to complete the pieced top.

Step 5. Cut and piece two 6½" x 83⅜" K strips green print; sew a strip to opposite long sides of the pieced center. Press seams toward strips.

Step 6. Sew an L strip set aside in Step 1 of Making Strip-Pieced

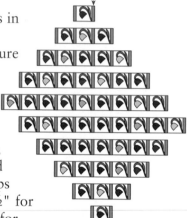

Figure 11
Arrange blocks in diagonal rows with D sashing strips.

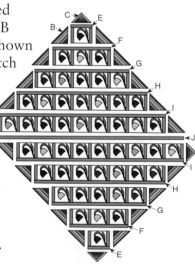

Figure 12
Arrange block rows with E–J strips and B and C triangles.

Triangles to the top and bottom of the pieced center. Press seams toward strips.

Finishing the Quilt

Step 1. Sandwich batting between the completed top and prepared backing piece; pin or baste layers together to hold flat for quilting.

Step 2. Quilt as desired by hand or machine. *Note: The quilt shown was professionally machine-quilted in an allover design using white machine-quilting thread.*

Step 3. When quilting is complete, trim batting and backing even with quilted top; remove pins or basting. Round corners using a plate as a pattern if desired.

Step 4. Cut nine 2¼" by fabric width strips green Bali print; join strips on short ends to make one long strip for binding.

Step 5. Fold the binding strip in half along length with wrong sides together; press.

Step 6. Bind edges referring to the General Instructions. ❖

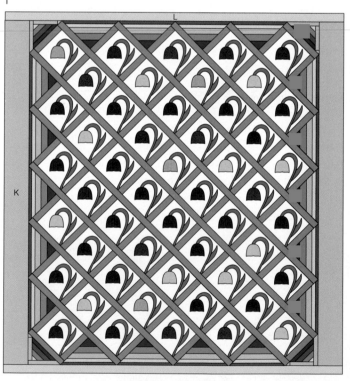

Nodding Tulips
Placement Diagram
Approximately 82" x 87"

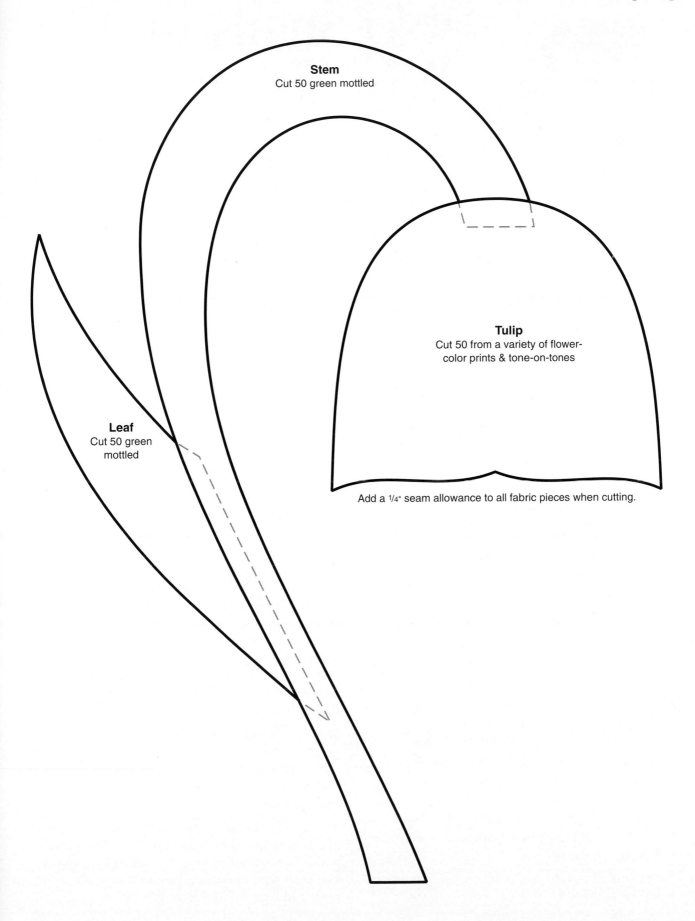

Stem
Cut 50 green mottled

Tulip
Cut 50 from a variety of flower-
color prints & tone-on-tones

Leaf
Cut 50 green
mottled

Add a ¼" seam allowance to all fabric pieces when cutting.

No Snails in My Garden

By Sue Harvey

Snail's Trail Variation blocks pair with appliquéd flowers to make this bright twin-size quilt.

Trim-and-Turn Appliqué

Jumbo rickrack stitched around the edge of each flower and flower center is used as a guide to turn the edges under for appliqué. Spray-on fusible web makes short work of fusing the leaf and vine pieces.

- Bright variegated and bright green Sulky rayon thread
- 3 yards Pellon Stitch-n-Tear fabric stabilizer
- 9 packages Wrights rainbow painted jumbo rickrack
- 505 Spray and Fix temporary adhesive spray
- 606 Spray and Fix spray-on fusible web
- DK5 adhesive spray cleaner
- Bo-Nash Giant Non-Stick Ironing & Craft Sheet
- Basic sewing tools and supplies

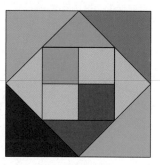

Snail's Trail Variation
7" x 7" Block

Project Specifications

Skill Level: Intermediate
Quilt Size: 63" x 82¾"
Block Size: 7" x 7"
Number of Blocks: 17

Materials

- ¼ yard dark blue vine print
- ¼ yard each pink and blue tiny florals
- ½ yard each pink and blue vine prints
- ½ yard dark green leaf print
- 1 yard light green leaf print
- 1 yard light green vine print
- 2 yards each light green, pink and blue florals
- Batting 70" x 90"
- Backing 70" x 90"
- Green all-purpose thread

Cutting

Step 1. Cut one strip each pink and blue vine prints and two strips light green vine print 2¼" by fabric width for A.

Step 2. Cut one strip each pink and blue vine prints and two strips light green vine print 3⅜" by fabric width; subcut strips into 3⅜" square segments. Cut each square on one diagonal to make 17 each pink and blue and 34 light green B triangles.

Step 3. Cut one strip each pink and blue florals and two strips light green floral 4⅜" by fabric width; subcut strips into 4⅜" square segments. Cut each square on one diagonal to make 17 each pink and blue and 34 light green C triangles.

Step 4. Cut two strips each pink and blue florals, three strips light green floral and four strips light green leaf print 7½" by fabric width; subcut strips into 7½" square segments for D. You will need six each pink and blue, 12 light green floral and 18 light green leaf print D squares.

Step 5. Cut two squares each pink and blue florals and three squares light green floral 11¼" x 11¼"; cut each square on both diagonals to yield five each pink and blue and 10 light green E triangles. Set aside remaining triangles for another project.

Step 6. Cut one square each pink, blue and light green florals 5⅞" x 5⅞"; cut each square on one diagonal to yield one each pink and blue and two light green F triangles. Set aside remaining triangles for another project.

Piecing Blocks

Step 1. Sew a pink A strip to a light green A strip with right sides together along length to make a strip set; press seam toward pink strip. Repeat with blue and light green A strips.

Step 2. Subcut strip sets into 2¼" A segments as shown in Figure 1. You will need 17 segments of each color combination.

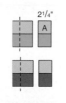
Figure 1
Subcut strip sets into 2¼" A segments.

Step 3. Sew a blue/light green A segment to a pink/light green A segment to make a Four-Patch unit as shown in Figure 2; repeat for 17 Four-Patch units.

Figure 2
Complete a Four-Patch unit as shown.

Step 4. Sew a light green B triangle to opposite sides of each Four-Patch unit as shown in Figure

3; add one each pink and blue B triangles to the remaining sides of each Four-Patch unit, again referring to Figure 3.

Figure 3
Sew B triangles
to each side of a
Four-Patch unit.

Step 5. Repeat Step 4 with C triangles to complete 17 Snail's Trail Variation blocks as shown in Figure 4.

Figure 4
Sew C triangles to each
side to complete 1 block.

Making Appliquéd Setting Squares & Border Strips

Step 1. Cut two border strips each 5½" x 20½" and 5½" x 40½" light green vine print.

Step 2. Prepare templates for G–L pieces; cut as directed on each piece except L leaf pieces.

Step 3. Place jumbo rickrack right sides together on the outer edge of each G–K piece as shown in Figure 5, overlapping beginning and end; stitch in place around center of rickrack.

Figure 5
Place jumbo rickrack
on the outer edge.

Step 4. Turn rickrack edge of each G–K piece under, leaving only half of rickrack exposed as shown in Figure 6; press.

Figure 6
Turn rickrack edge under,
leaving half of rickrack exposed.

Step 5. Lightly spray wrong side of dark green leaf

print with spray-on fusible web; let dry. ***Note:** Use adhesive spray cleaner to remove any over spray on work surface after applying spray-on fusible web and temporary adhesive spray.*

Step 6. Draw two undulating lines 36" long and no more than 3" wide on the wrong side of the sprayed fabric as shown in Figure 7. Draw echoing lines about ¾"–1" away from the first lines to make vines as shown in Figure 8. Repeat to make two 16" long vines.

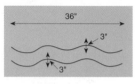

Figure 7
Draw 2 undulating lines 36" long
and no more than 3" wide.

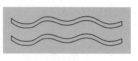

Figure 8
Draw echoing lines ¾"–1" away
from the first lines to make vines.

Step 7. Trace 62 L pieces around the vines on the wrong side of the sprayed fabric; cut out leaves and vines.

Step 8. Arrange two or three leaves on each light green leaf print D square, a long vine and six leaves on each long border strip, and a short vine and four leaves on each short border strip referring to Figure 9 for positioning suggestions.

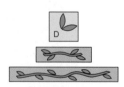

Figure 9
Arrange leaves and vines on the
D squares and border strips.

Step 9. Place flowers on the D squares and border strips referring to the Placement Diagram for positioning.

Step 10. Rearrange leaves and vines under flowers until satisfied with positioning; remove flowers. Place non-stick ironing sheet over leaves and vines; fuse in place with medium dry iron following manufacturer's instructions.

Step 11. Straight-stitch close to edge of leaf and vine pieces and to make vein lines on leaves using bright green rayon thread in the top of the machine and all-purpose thread in the bobbin.

Step 12. Lightly spray the wrong side of each K piece with temporary adhesive spray; center a sprayed K piece on each G–J piece.

Step 13. Lightly spray the wrong side of each flower with temporary adhesive spray; place flowers on the D squares and border strips and press in place with fingers to hold.

Step 14. Straight-stitch on rickrack close to edge of flower and center pieces using bright variegated rayon thread in the top of the machine and all-purpose thread in the bobbin to complete the D setting squares and appliquéd border strips.

Completing the Top

Step 1. Arrange pieced blocks with appliquéd D setting squares, pink, blue and light green D squares and E and F triangles as shown in Figure 10; join pieces in rows. Join rows to complete the center.

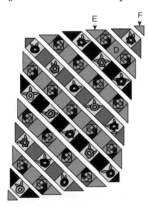

Figure 10
Arrange pieced blocks with D squares and E and F triangles.

Step 2. Cut and piece two strips each 2¼" x 53½" and 2¼" x 69¾" light green floral. Sew the longer strips to opposite long sides of the pieced center and the shorter strips to the top and bottom; press seams toward strips.

Step 3. Cut four strips each 5½" x 16⅞" and 5½" x 17" pink floral. Sew an 16⅞"-long strip to each end of the longer appliquéd border strips; sew a pieced strip to opposite long sides of the

No Snails in My Garden
Placement Diagram
63" x 82¾"

pieced center; press seams toward strips. Sew a 17"-long strip to each end of the shorter appliquéd border strips; sew a pieced strip to the top and bottom of the pieced center to complete the top; press seams toward strips.

Finishing the Quilt

Step 1. Sandwich the batting between the prepared backing and completed top; pin or baste to hold.

Step 2. Quilt as desired by hand or machine. *Note: The sample shown was professionally machine-quilted.*

Step 3. Remove pins or basting; trim edges even with the quilted top.

Step 4. Cut eight strips 2¼" by fabric width blue floral; join strips on short ends to make a long strip. Press strip in half with wrong sides together to make a binding strip. Bind edges of quilt to finish. ❖

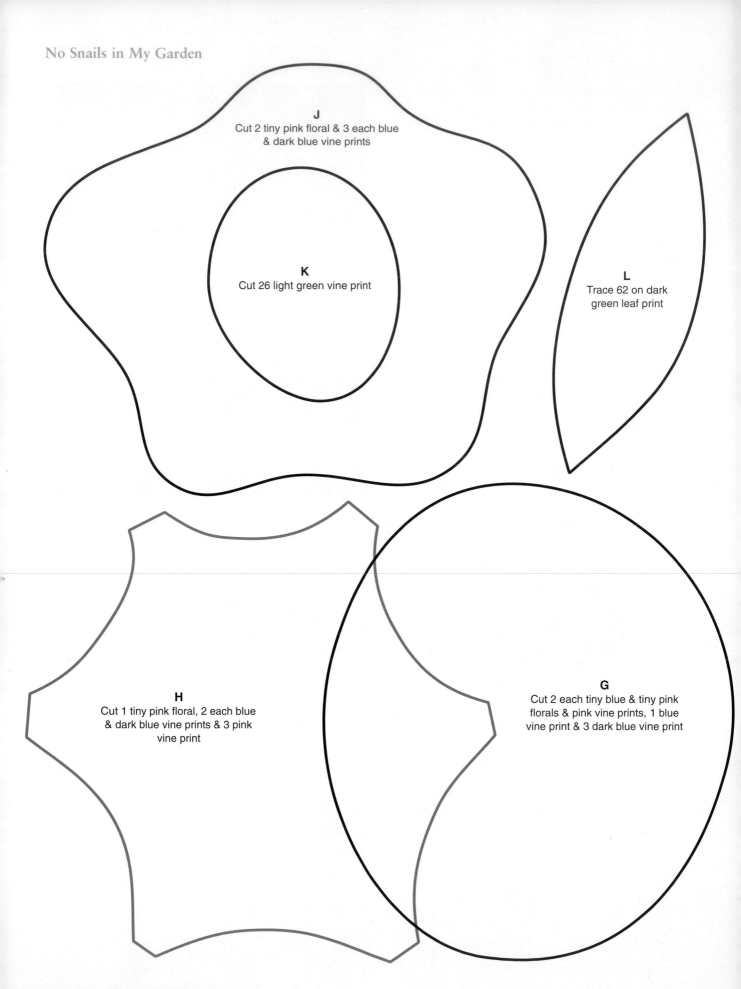

J
Cut 2 tiny pink floral & 3 each blue
& dark blue vine prints

K
Cut 26 light green vine prints

L
Trace 62 on dark
green leaf print

H
Cut 1 tiny pink floral, 2 each blue
& dark blue vine prints & 3 pink
vine print

G
Cut 2 each tiny blue & tiny pink
florals & pink vine prints, 1 blue
vine print & 3 dark blue vine print

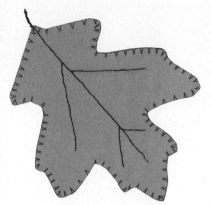

My Favorite Season Penny Rug

By Carla G. Schwab

Stitch up a quick decorative accent using popular wool-felt techniques.

Felt Appliqué

Because felt will not ravel, it does not require seams or any application to preserve the edges. Simply place the shapes and stitch to complete a quick project.

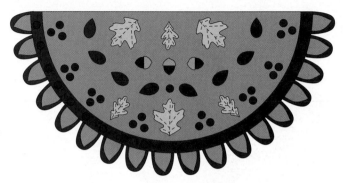

My Favorite Season Penny Rug
Placement Diagram
36" x 18½"

Project Specifications
Skill Level: Beginner
Rug Size: 36" x 18½"

Materials
- 1 piece each 12" x 18" gold, red, brown and tan wool felt
- 1 yard light green wool felt
- 1½ yards dark green wool felt
- 1 spool heavyweight brown thread
- 1 skein brown 6-strand embroidery floss
- Basic sewing tools and supplies

Instructions

Step 1. Cut one half circle 17" deep by 33" wide light green wool felt for M.

Step 2. Cut two half circles 18½" deep by 36" wide dark green wool felt for N.

Step 3. Prepare templates using patterns given; cut as directed on each piece.

Step 4. Pin or baste appliqué pieces A–F onto M referring to the Placement Diagram for positioning.

Step 5. Using heavyweight brown thread, machine-stitch each piece in place using a blind hemstitch.

Step 6. Using 2 strands brown embroidery floss, hand-stitch leaf details using a backstitch referring to patterns for placement.

Step 7. Pin or baste the remaining A berries evenly spaced ¼" from the round edge of one N; stitch in place as in Step 5.

Step 8. Layer the appliquéd M piece right side up on the appliquéd N piece, matching straight edges; stitch along the rounded edge of M as in Step 5 to attach layers.

Step 9. Pin or baste the G pieces to the H pieces, placing straight edge of G ¼" inside straight edge of H as shown in Figure 1. Stitch around curved edges of G as in Step 5.

Figure 1
Pin or baste a G piece to H
with straight edge of G ¼"
inside straight edge of H.

Step 10. Place an H piece on the wrong side of each G-H unit; stitch around the curved H edges as in Step 5.

Step 11. Pin the straight edge of the G-H units to the backside curved edge of the appliquéd M-N layers as shown in Figure 2, evenly spacing the units around the curved edge; baste to hold.

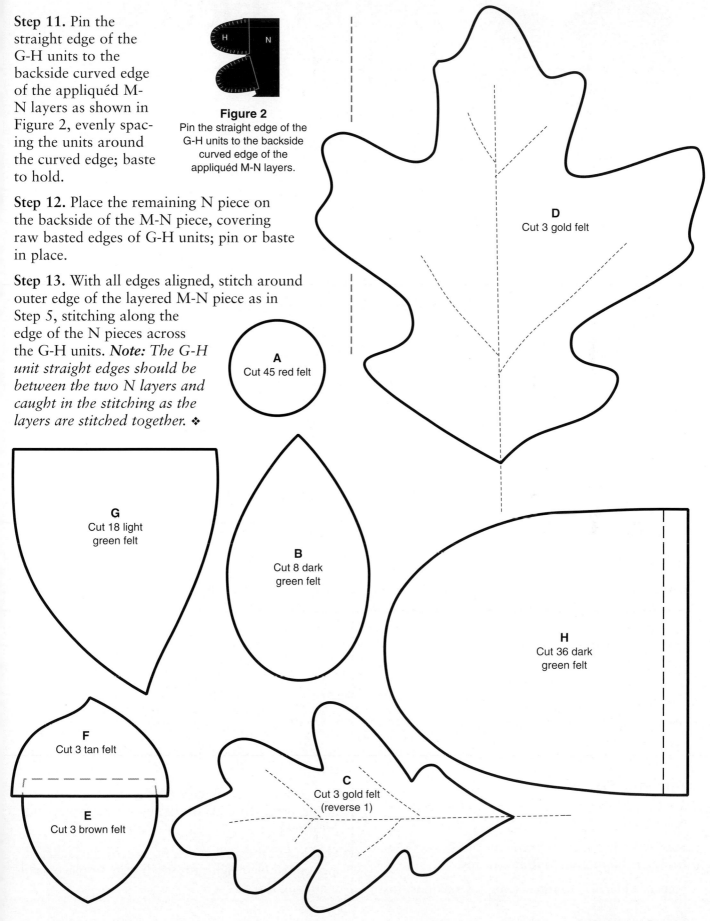

Figure 2
Pin the straight edge of the G-H units to the backside curved edge of the appliquéd M-N layers.

Step 12. Place the remaining N piece on the backside of the M-N piece, covering raw basted edges of G-H units; pin or baste in place.

Step 13. With all edges aligned, stitch around outer edge of the layered M-N piece as in Step 5, stitching along the edge of the N pieces across the G-H units. *Note: The G-H unit straight edges should be between the two N layers and caught in the stitching as the layers are stitched together.* ❖

D
Cut 3 gold felt

A
Cut 45 red felt

G
Cut 18 light green felt

B
Cut 8 dark green felt

H
Cut 36 dark green felt

F
Cut 3 tan felt

E
Cut 3 brown felt

C
Cut 3 gold felt
(reverse 1)

Berber Fleece Jacket

By Chris Malone

Appliquéd flowers adorn this warm Berber fleece jacket.

Appliqué on Textured Fabric

To appliqué shapes to a very textured fabric such as this Berber fleece jacket, fuse a lightweight interfacing to fabrics before cutting to add body and to control fraying.

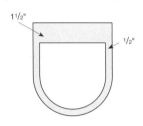

Project Specifications

Skill Level: Beginner

Jacket Size: Size varies

Materials

- Completed jacket (the sample is made using Berber fleece with a blanket-stitch edge finish)
- 7" x 8" piece tan homespun for pocket
- Assorted scraps of blue, orange, rust, gold, and green for appliqués
- Tan and green all-purpose thread
- Black 6-strand embroidery floss
- 5 (½"–⅞") assorted color buttons
- Fray preventative
- Pellon No. 911FF lightweight fusible interfacing
- Basic sewing tools and supplies

Appliqué Preparation

Note: Use 2 strands of black embroidery floss for all handstitching.

Step 1. Using pattern given, cut out pocket shape from tan homespun and interfacing.

Step 2. Referring to interfacing instructions, fuse to the wrong side of the fabric pocket, leaving a ½" margin around sides and bottom of pocket and 1½" at top as shown in Figure 1.

Figure 1
Fuse the lightweight interfacing to the wrong side of the fabric pocket, leaving a ½" margin around sides and bottom of pocket and 1½" at top.

Step 3. Press and sew ¼" hem along the top of the pocket. Fold the upper edge of the pocket to the right side along the interfacing line to create a facing as shown in Figure 2. Stitch along outer edges of folded section with a ½" seam allowance.

Figure 2
Fold the upper edge of the pocket to the right side along the interfacing line; stitch along outer edges of folded section with a ½" seam as shown.

Step 4. Trim corners and turn facing to the wrong side; press.

Step 5. Fold the raw edges of the pocket to the inside along the edge of the fused interfacing and press well.

Step 6. Pin the pocket to one side of the jacket at a comfortable height; topstitch edge in place using matching thread.

Berber Fleece Jacket

Step 7. Trace five leaf shapes onto the wrong side of green scraps; fold each scrap in half with right sides together with traced pattern on top and pin to secure. Sew on the marked lines as shown in Figure 3.

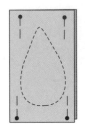

Figure 3
Sew on the
marked lines.

Step 8. Cut out each leaf shape ⅛" from stitched line; trim tip and clip curves.

Step 9. Cut a slash through one layer only; turn right side out through slash. Smooth curves and pull out points; press. Apply fray preventative to cut edges; let dry. Whipstitch slash opening closed.

Step 10. For flowers, trace flower shapes on untreated side of the lightweight fusible interfacing, leaving about ½" between each piece. Cut out between shapes, leaving a ¼" margin. Fuse shapes to the wrong side of fabrics as directed on patterns for color; cut out on traced lines.

Step 11. Pin flower centers to flowers matching large and small flowers with the appropriate size center. Blanket-stitch around edges.

Step 12. Pin one large and two small flower motifs and three leaves above pocket area, referring to the Placement Diagram for positioning suggestions. Repeat on the opposite jacket front in the shoulder area with one each large and small

Berber Fleece Jacket
Placement Diagram
Size Varies

flower and two leaves, again referring to the Placement Diagram.

Step 13. Blanket-stitch around each flower shape to attach to jacket.

Step 14. To attach leaves, sew five fly stitches down the center of each leaf, sewing through leaf and jacket fabric as shown in Figure 4. *Note: Edges of leaves will be loose.*

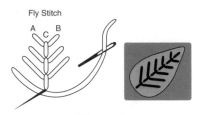

Figure 4
Sew 5 fly stitches down the
center of each leaf, sewing
through leaf and jacket fabric.

Step 15. Sew a button to the center of each flower motif to finish. ❖

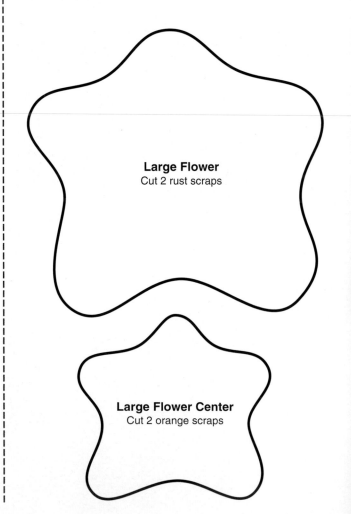

Large Flower
Cut 2 rust scraps

Large Flower Center
Cut 2 orange scraps

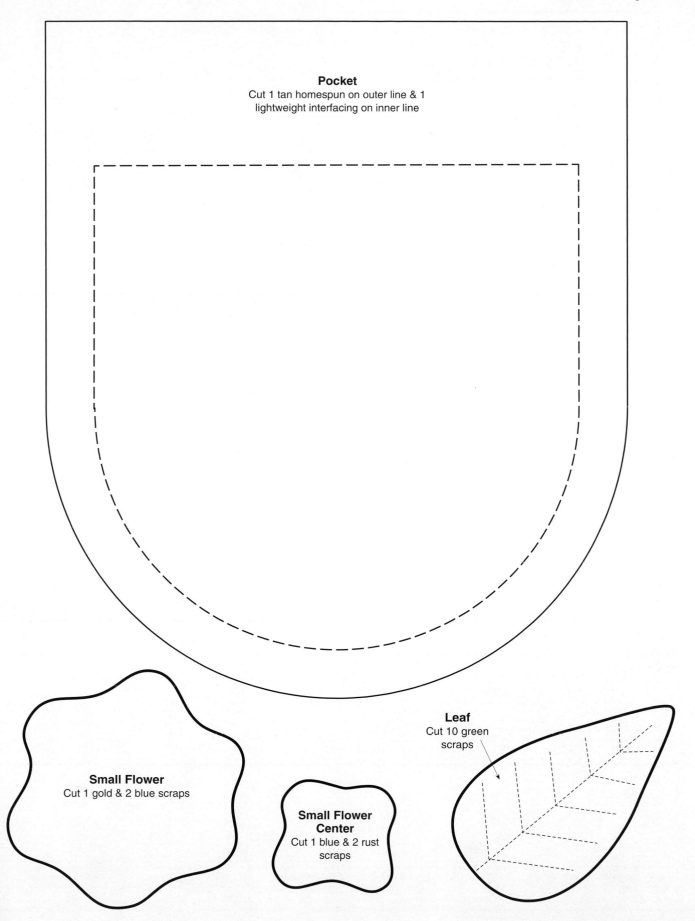

Pocket
Cut 1 tan homespun on outer line & 1
lightweight interfacing on inner line

Small Flower
Cut 1 gold & 2 blue scraps

**Small Flower
Center**
Cut 1 blue & 2 rust
scraps

Leaf
Cut 10 green
scraps

Picture Perfect

Wildflower Bouquet

By Sue Harvey

Use a variety of 3-D techniques to make this just-picked-fresh bouquet of summer flowers.

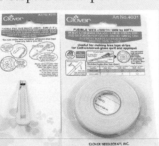
Project Specifications

Skill Level: Intermediate
Quilt Size: 34" x 34"

Materials

- ⅛ yard each yellow and pink mottleds
- ¼ yard each medium green and purple mottleds
- ⅓ yard each dark green mottled and multicolor print
- ⅜ yard each white-on-white print and light green floral
- ⅝ yard each medium green and pink florals and light green solid
- Batting 38" x 38"
- Backing 38" x 38"
- All-purpose thread to match fabrics
- Light green machine-quilting thread
- Yellow 6-strand embroidery floss

- ½ yard Wonder-Under fusible web
- 3 yards Clover ¼"-wide fusible web
- ½ yard Stitch-n-Tear fabric stabilizer
- 505 Spray & Fix basting spray
- ¼" fusible bias maker
- Polyester fiberfill
- Basic sewing tools and supplies

Completing the Top

Step 1. Cut four squares pink floral and two squares each light and medium green florals 9¼" x 9¼"; cut each square on both diagonals to make A triangles. You will need eight each light and medium green A triangles and 16 pink A triangles.

Step 2. Cut two squares pink floral 8⅞" x 8⅞"; cut each square on one diagonal to make four B triangles.

Step 3. Cut two squares light green floral 9⅞" x 9⅞"; cut each square on one diagonal to make four C triangles.

Step 4. Cut one square light green solid 16½" x 16½" for the center square.

Step 5. Join two medium green A triangles with one pink A triangle to make a strip as shown in Figure 1; press seams toward the medium green triangles. Repeat for four strips.

Figure 1
Join A triangles to make a strip.

Step 6. Center and sew a strip to each side of the center square as shown in Figure 2; press seams toward strips.

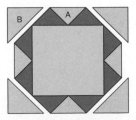

Figure 2
Sew a strip to each side of the center square; add B to each angled edge.

Step 7. Sew a B triangle to each angled edge of the pieced section, again referring to Figure 2; press seams toward B.

Step 8. Cut two strips each 1½" x 24½" and 1½" x 26½" multicolor print. Sew the shorter strips to opposite sides of the pieced section and the longer strips to the remaining sides; press seams toward strips.

Step 9. Join two light green A triangles with three pink A triangles to make a strip as shown in Figure 3; press seams in one direction. Repeat for four strips.

Figure 3
Join A triangles to make a strip.

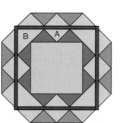

Figure 4
Sew a strip to each side
of the pieced section.

Step 10. Center and sew a strip to each side of the pieced section as shown in Figure 4; press seams toward the multicolor print strips.

Step 11. Trim the multicolor print strips even with the angled edges of the pink A triangles as shown in Figure 5.

Figure 5
Trim the multicolor print strips
even with the angled edges of A.

Step 12. Sew a light green C triangle to each angled edge of the pieced section to complete the top referring to the Placement Diagram; press seams toward C.

Step 13. Apply basting spray to one side of the batting square; position on the backing square and smooth. Apply basting spray to the remaining side of the batting square; center the completed top on the batting and smooth.

Step 14. Machine-quilt a 1" crosshatch grid on the center square, 1" from seams on the A, B and C triangles and in the ditch of seams of the multicolor print strips using light green machine-

quilting thread in the top of the machine and all-purpose thread in the bobbin.

Step 15. Trim batting and backing even with the quilted top. Cut four strips 2½" by fabric width medium green floral. Join strips on short ends to make a long strip; press in half along length with wrong sides together. Bind edges of quilt.

Making Stems and Ribbon

Step 1. Cut a 1½" x 18" strip multicolor print; turn under long edges ¼" and press.

Step 2. Fold each end in at an angle as shown in Figure 6; press. Press strip in half along length; stitch across ends and along length to make ribbon piece.

Figure 6
Fold each end in at an angle.

Step 3. Cut and join ½"-wide dark green mottled bias strips on short ends to make a 94"-long strip.

Step 4. Use the ¼" fusible bias maker to make ¼"-wide bias and apply ¼"-wide fusible web to the strip; remove paper backing. ***Note:*** *To make bias without a bias maker, turn under each long edge of the bias strip ⅛" and press. Apply ¼"-wide fusible web to the back of the strip.*

Step 5. Cut the following stem pieces from the bias strip: one 13", two 12", one 11", three 10", two 9" and one 6". Turn one end of each piece under ⅛" for bottom end.

Step 6. Arrange the ribbon and stem pieces on the center square as shown in Figure 7; fuse stem pieces in place.

Figure 7
Arrange the ribbon and
stem pieces as shown.

Step 7. Stitch close to edge all around each stem piece using dark green all-purpose thread.

Step 8. Tie ribbon ends in knot at edge of stems. Arrange ends to lie flat and stitch along bottom edge of each piece to hold in place.

Making Leaves

Step 1. Prepare templates for the leaf shapes.

Step 2. Cut a 7" x 9" piece medium green mottled; fold in half with right sides together.

Step 3. Trace two D shapes leaving ½" between shapes. Stitch around each leaf shape on the marked lines as shown in Figure 8; cut out each shape leaving a ⅛" seam allowance beyond the stitched line.

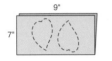

Figure 8
Stitch around each leaf shape on the marked lines.

Figure 9
Cut a slit in the leaf shapes.

Step 4. Cut a slit in one side of one shape for D. Reverse the second shape for DR and cut as for D as shown in Figure 9; turn shapes right side out through slits. Slipstitch opening closed; press flat.

Step 5. Fold the remaining medium green mottled in half with wrong sides together. Trace one each E, F, G, H and J leaves on the folded fabric.

Step 6. Cut out shapes on the marked lines through both layers. Cut a piece of tear-off fabric stabilizer to fit behind each shape. Pin each layered fabric shape to the stabilizer piece.

Step 7. Using a close medium-width stitch, satin-stitch around edge of each shape through all layers using all-purpose thread to match fabrics, as shown in Figure 10. Remove stabilizer.

Figure 10
Satin-stitch around edge of each shape.

Step 8. Arrange leaf shapes on stems as shown

in Figure 11. Stitch a center vein line on each leaf to attach to the quilt leaving ends free as shown in Figure 12.

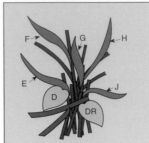

Figure 11
Arrange leaf shapes on stems.

Figure 12
Stitch a center vein on each leaf.

Making Daisies

Step 1. Cut the following white-on-white print strips: four 4" x 13" for large daisies, two 3½" x 11" for small daisy and four 3½" x 8" for half daisies.

Step 2. Cut the following strips fusible web: two 3" x 13" for large daisies, one 2½" x 11 for small daisy and two 2½" x 8" for half daisies.

Step 3. To make a large daisy, center and fuse one strip fusible web to the wrong side of one white-on-white print strip, leaving ½" unfused along both edges; remove paper backing. Fuse to the wrong side of another white-on-white print strip.

Step 4. Fold fused strip in half along length; press.

Step 5. Draw a line ½" from the raw edge on one side of the folded strip as shown in Figure 13.

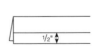

Figure 13
Draw a line ½" from raw edge on 1 side of the folded strip.

Figure 14
Cut the folded edge into strips.

Step 6. Cut the folded edge into strips about ¼" wide using a rotary cutter or scissors and cutting only to the drawn line as shown in Figure 14.

Step 7. Sew a gathering stitch through both layers along the ½" uncut edge as shown in Figure 15; pull to gather strip. Hand-stitch ends of strip to form

Figure 15
Sew a gathering stitch along the uncut edge.

a circle as shown in Figure 16; trim excess unfused fabric in circle center to reduce bulk.

Figure 16
Hand-stitch ends of strip to form a circle.

Figure 17
Join ends of gathered strip to make a double-layer strip.

Step 8. Repeat Steps 3–7 to make two large daisies, one small daisy and two half daisies. ***Note:*** *Half daisies will not form a circle; join ends of gathered strip to make a double-layer strip as shown in Figure 17.*

Step 9. Prepare template for K; cut as directed on the pattern.

Step 10. Sew a gathering stitch ⅛" from edge around one yellow mottled circle; pull to gather loosely as shown in Figure 18. Insert small amount of polyester fiberfill into opening.

Figure 18
Pull to loosely gather circle.

Step 11. Place stuffed circle over center of one large daisy; hand-stitch in place. Repeat with all yellow mottled circles on the large and small daisies.

Step 12. Turn under ⅛" around edge of one medium green mottled circle. Sew a gathering stitch around the edge; gather slightly. Insert unfused edges of a half-daisy piece into the gathered circle; gather tightly around daisy piece to form base. Hand-stitch top edge of base to daisy piece. Repeat for second half daisy.

Step 13. Arrange daisies on stem pieces referring to the Placement Diagram for positioning. Hand-stitch in place through top and batting layers of quilt only.

Making Pansies

Step 1. Cut two strips pink mottled 3½" x 14". Fold each strip in half along length with wrong sides together; press.

Step 2. Use a doubled thread to hand-stitch a gathering stitch along the length of the folded strip in the pattern shown in Figure 19; pull to gather strip into five petals as shown in Figure 20.

Step 3. Arrange two petals for pansy back petals;

Wildflower Bouquet
Placement Diagram
34" x 34"

Figure 19
Hand-stitch a gathering stitch along length of strip as shown.

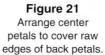

Figure 20
Gather strip into 5 petals.

twist strip and arrange two petals for center petals, covering raw edges of back petals with center petals as shown in Figure 21.

Figure 21
Arrange center petals to cover raw edges of back petals.

Figure 22
Cover raw edges of center petals with front petal.

Step 4. Twist strip and arrange front petal, placing raw edge of front petal under center petals and covering raw edges of center petals with front petal as shown in Figure 22.

Step 5. Hand-stitch petals on back to hold in place. Repeat for second pansy.

Step 6. Use 6 strands yellow embroidery floss to make three or four loops between center and front petals of each pansy.

Step 7. Arrange pansies on stems referring to the Placement Diagram for positioning. Hand-stitch in place through top and batting layers of quilt only.

Making Violets

Step 1. Prepare template for L; trace three circles on purple mottled. Cut out, leaving ¼" all around each circle.

Step 2. Sew a gathering stitch on the traced line. Gather tightly and knot, do not cut thread; flatten into a circle.

Step 3. Bring needle to top at center of circle; go around one edge to back of circle and up through center as shown in Figure 23. Pull to gather edge in as shown in Figure 24. Repeat on opposite edge as shown in Figure 25.

Figure 23
Go around 1 edge to back
and up through center.

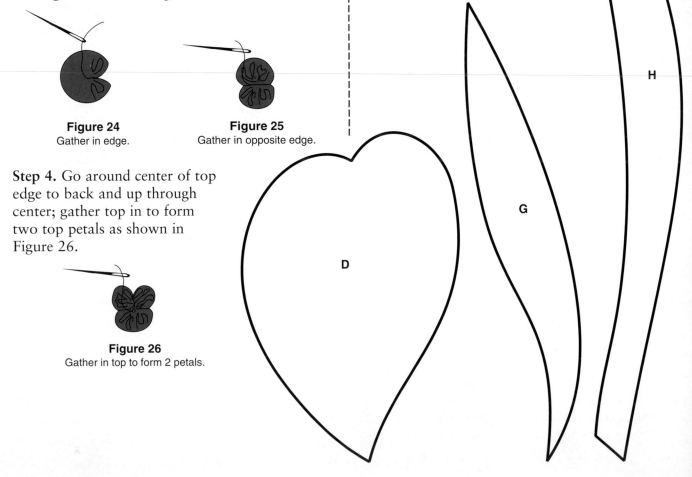

Figure 24
Gather in edge.

Figure 25
Gather in opposite edge.

Step 4. Go around center of top edge to back and up through center; gather top in to form two top petals as shown in Figure 26.

Figure 26
Gather in top to form 2 petals.

Step 5. Divide and gather bottom half of circle into three petals as shown in Figure 27 to complete one violet; knot and cut thread. Repeat to make three violets.

Step 6. Use 6 strands yellow embroidery floss to make three French knots in the center of each violet.

Step 7. Arrange violets on stems referring to the Placement Diagram for positioning. Hand-stitch in place through top and batting layers of quilt only to finish. ❖

Figure 27
Divide and gather
bottom half into 3 petals.

D

G

H

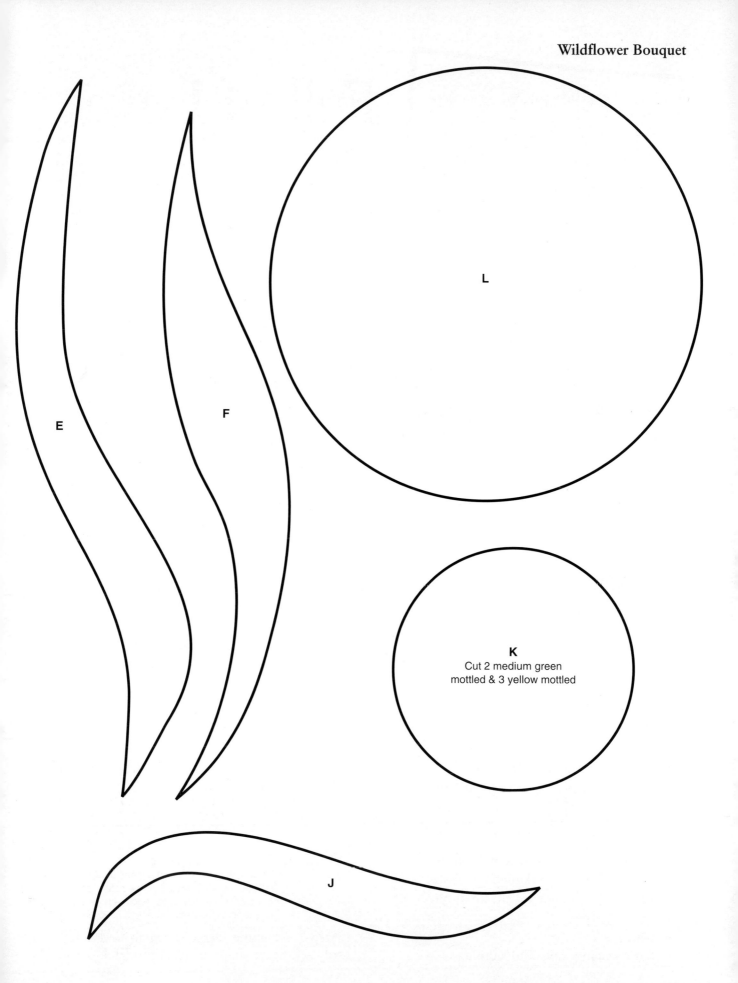

E

F

L

K
Cut 2 medium green
mottled & 3 yellow mottled

J

Full of Love

By Holly Daniels

Send a message of love with this little wall quilt.

Project Specifications

Skill Level: Beginner

Quilt Size: 18½" x 12½"

Materials

- 15" x 9" rectangle white-on-white print for background
- 3 (6" x 8") rectangles light pink tone-on-tones for hearts
- 8" x 16" rectangle medium green print for letters
- ¼ yard green floral for borders
- ¼ yard dark pink tone-on-tone for flat piping and binding
- Backing 23" x 17"
- Batting 23" x 17"
- All-purpose thread to match fabrics
- Clear nylon monofilament
- 15" x 9" rectangle fabric stabilizer
- Freezer paper
- Glue stick
- Basic sewing tools and supplies

Appliqué

Step 1. Trace three hearts and the letters onto the dull paper side of the freezer paper. ***Note:*** *The letters will be reversed at this time.* Cut out on traced lines.

Step 2. Place each shape with waxy side down, on the wrong side of medium green print; press lightly with a warm, dry iron to adhere. Cut out, leaving a ¼" margin all around, including in the center of the letter O.

Step 3. Fold raw edges of each piece over edge of freezer paper and use a glue stick to adhere fabric to the paper side of the freezer paper; let dry.

Step 4. Thread sewing machine with clear nylon monofilament in the top of the machine and all-purpose thread in the bobbin. Set stitch to a very narrow zigzag.

Step 5. Pin the 15" x 9" rectangle fabric stabilizer behind the background rectangle.

Step 6. Place the two outer heart shapes on the background with edges approximately 1¼" from each side edge of the background and overlapping the center heart shape area referring to Figure 1 and the Placement Diagram and project photo for positioning.

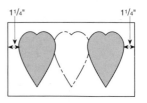

Figure 1
Place the 2 outer heart shapes on the background with edges approximately 1¼" from each side edge of the background and overlapping the center heart shape area.

Step 7. Machine zigzag-stitch around outer edges of each heart shape to secure to background.

Step 8. Remove fabric stabilizer; cut a small hole through the background behind one heart shape. Trim backing fabric to within ¼" of inner heart edges as shown in Figure 2.

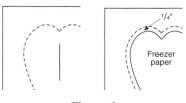

Figure 2
Cut a small hole through the background behind 1 heart shape. Trim backing fabric to within ¼" of inner heart edges.

Step 9. Loosen the glued-down edges of heart away from freezer paper; remove freezer paper. Press from the backside to avoid overheating the clear nylon monofilament stitches. Repeat with the second heart shape.

Step 10. Place the center heart over the two stitched hearts and appliqué in place as in Step 7. Cut away fabric from the backside as in Step 8,

cutting away portions that overlap previous appliqué work.

Step 11. Place letters across the appliquéd hearts referring to the Placement Diagram for positioning. Appliqué in place as in Step 7; remove freezer paper as in Step 9.

Completing the Top

Step 1. Cut two 2" x 10" A strips and two 2" x 16" B strips dark pink tone-on-tone.

Step 2. Fold each A and B strip in half along length with wrong sides together to make flat piping; press.

Step 3. Measuring from folded side, trim each strip to ½" wide as shown in Figure 3; trim A strips to 9" long and B strips to 15" long.

Figure 3
Trim strips to ½" wide.

Step 4. Lay an A strip on one short edge of the appliquéd top, matching raw edges as shown

Full of Love

in Figure 4; baste in place. Repeat with second A strip on opposite short end and B strips on the top and bottom.

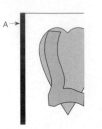

Figure 4
Lay an A strip on 1 short edge of the appliquéd top, matching raw edges.

Step 5. Cut two 2½" x 9" C strips and two 2½" x 19" D strips green floral. Sew C to opposite short sides and D to the top and bottom of the appliquéd center; press seams toward strips.

Finishing the Quilt

Step 1. Sandwich batting between the completed top and prepared backing piece; pin or baste layers together to hold flat for quilting.

Step 2. Quilt as desired by hand or machine. *Note: The quilt shown was machine-quilted in a meandering pattern in the background, on the hearts and in the borders using clear nylon monofilament in the top of the machine and all-purpose thread in the bobbin.*

Step 3. When quilting is complete, trim batting and backing even with quilted top; remove pins or basting.

Step 4. Cut two 2¼" by fabric width strips dark pink tone-on-tone. Join strips on short ends to make one long strip for binding.

Step 5. Fold the binding strip in half along length with wrong sides together; press.

Step 6. Bind edges referring to the General Instructions. ❖

Full of Love
Placement Diagram
18½" x 12½"

Heart
Cut 3 light pink
tone-on-tones

Letters
Cut 1 each medium green print

Plants in My Window

By Connie Kauffman

Planting season is just around the corner every day with this fabric planting scene.

Raw-Edge Appliqué

Cut the appliqué shapes to size, glue the edges and stitch raw edges to the background using fabric glue. Adhere to the surface before stitching with spray adhesive. No turning or fusing is necessary. Quilting is completed as you sew.

Project Specifications

Skill Level: Beginner
Quilt Size: 18" x 15"

Materials

- 11½" x 11½" square blue for sky for A
- 2" x 11½" strip brown for B
- 2½" x 15" strip tan mottled for C
- 2½" x 15" strip brown mottled for D
- 4" x 13½" strip leaf print for E
- 4" x 13½" strip olive green for F
- 4" x 12" strip terra-cotta solid for pots
- ¼ yard wood-grain print for binding
- Scraps light, medium and dark green, rust, tan, charcoal and light, medium and dark gray mottleds or tone-on-tones
- Backing 22" x 19"
- Batting 22" x 19"
- All-purpose thread to match fabrics

- Sulky KK 2000 Spray Adhesive
- Aleene's Easy Flow Tacky Glue
- Basic sewing tools and supplies

Completing the Background

Step 1. Apply spray adhesive on the wrong side of the backing piece and place wrong side against batting.

Step 2. Apply spray adhesive to the wrong side of A; center A on the batting piece right side up.

Step 3. Place small dots of fabric glue along the edges of the back of B; place on A along the bottom edge matching the left corner. Stitch in place along top raw edge of B.

Step 4. Sew D to the A-B unit, stopping stitching 1" away from the edge of A as shown in Figure 1; press seam toward D.

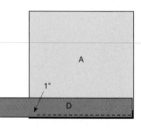

Figure 1
Sew D to the A-B unit, stopping stitching 1" away from the edge of A.

Step 5. Add E, then C and then F to the A-B-D unit, pressing seams toward strips after stitching. Complete the D seam as shown in Figure 2.

Step 6. Machine-baste around outer edges to secure. Trim backing and batting edges even with top.

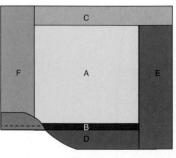

Figure 2
Complete the D seam.

Step 7. Fold and crease to mark the center of the background.

Appliqué

Step 1. Prepare templates for appliqué shapes using the full-size pattern given. Trace shapes on the right side of the fabrics as directed on each piece for color.

Step 2. Cut out shapes on the marked lines.

Step 3. Apply small dots of fabric glue along the edges on the wrong side of the number 1 appliqué piece; place on the quilt top referring to center marks on pattern and crease lines on background for placement.

Step 4. Apply glue and arrange all pieces in numerical order, overlapping pieces as necessary.

Step 5. Using all-purpose thread to match fabric, stitch close to the edge of each piece; add detail lines to leaves as desired.

Finishing

Step 1. Quilt as desired by hand or machine. *Note: The quilt shown was machine-quilted in a meandering pattern to resemble rocks in D, in diagonal lines spaced 2" apart on E and F, and in straight lines on C using all-purpose thread to match fabrics.*

Step 2. Cut two 2¼" by fabric width strips wood-grain print. Join strips on short ends to make one long strip for binding.

Step 3. Fold the binding strip in half along length with wrong sides together; press.

Step 4. Bind edges referring to the General Instructions. ❖

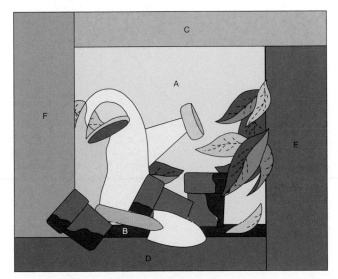

Plants in My Window
Placement Diagram
18" x 15"

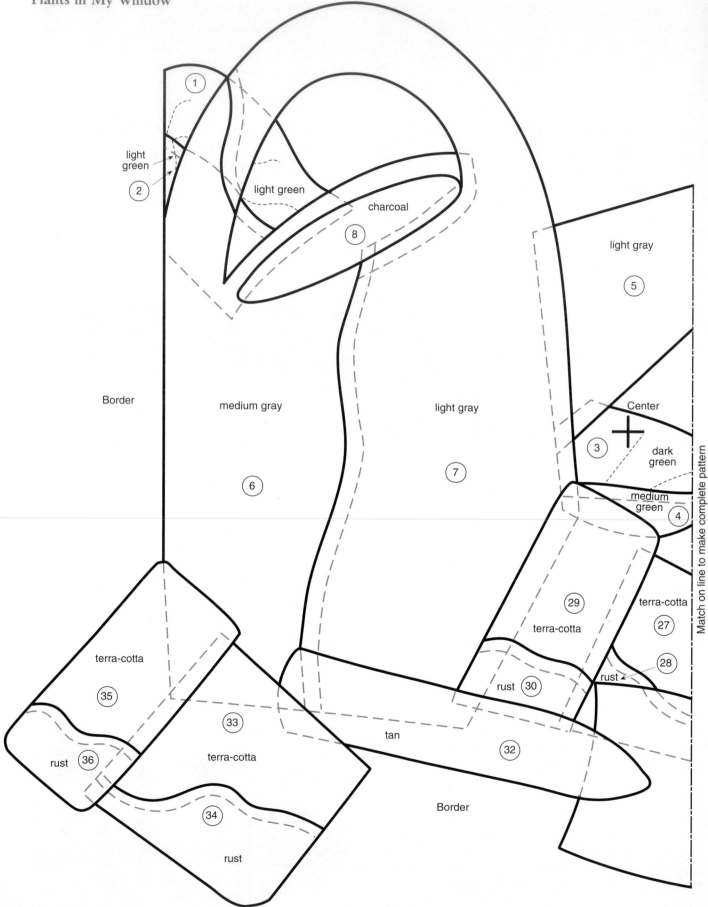

light green
2
light green
charcoal
8

Border
medium gray
6
light gray
7

light gray
5

Center
3
dark green
medium green
4

Match on line to make complete pattern

29
terra-cotta
27
terra-cotta
28
rust
rust 30

terra-cotta
35
33
tan
32
terra-cotta
34
rust 36
rust
Border

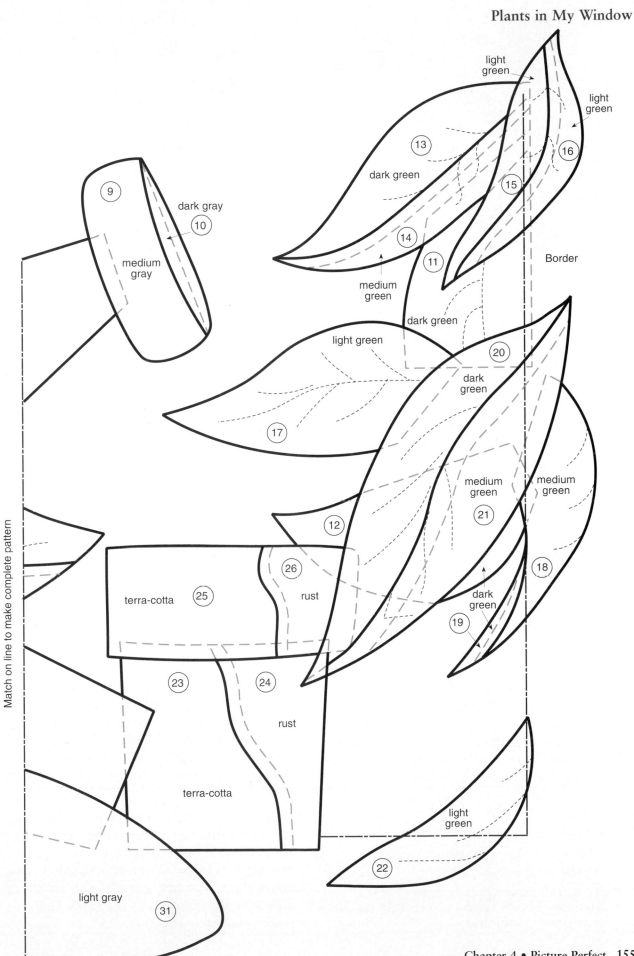

light
green

light
green

⑬

dark green

⑯

⑮

⑨

dark gray
⑩

medium
gray

⑭

⑪

medium
green

Border

dark green

light green

⑳

dark
green

⑰

medium
green

medium
green

⑫

㉑

⑱

⑲

dark
green

㉖

㉕ rust

terra-cotta

Match on line to make complete pattern

㉓

㉔

rust

terra-cotta

light
green

light gray

㉒

㉛

Fruit Bowl Watercolor

By Judith Sandstrom

A pieced background similar to a watercolor painting is the backdrop for the appliquéd motifs.

Fusible Appliqué on a Pieced Background

A fruit bowl filled with fabric fruit motifs is applied to a pieced background using a fusible interfacing printed with a 2" grid.

Project Specifications
Skill Level: Beginner
Quilt Size: 19" x 22"

Materials
- Scraps black, red, orange, yellow, gold, purple and green prints, solids or tone-on-tones for fruit appliqués
- Scraps of approximately 12 different light green and 16 different off-white/tan prints or tone-on-tones for background squares
- ¼ yard black print for binding
- ¼ yard black print for borders
- Backing 23" x 26"
- Batting 23" x 26"
- All-purpose thread to match fabrics
- ½ yard fusible web
- 20" x 24" piece Quilt-Fuse from HTC (Handler Textile Corp.) or other 2" fusible nonwoven layout grid

- Brown fine-point fabric marker
- Basic sewing tools and supplies

Piecing the Background
Step 1. Prewash and iron all fabrics before cutting.

Step 2. From each of the light green and off-white/tan scraps, cut four or five 2" x 2" squares. *Note: These do not have to be cut accurately and some will not actually be used.*

Step 3. Place the layout grid base on a heat-safe surface with the fusible side up and printed grid side down. *Note: Even with the print side down, the grid can easily be seen.*

Step 4. Arrange the 2" x 2" squares on the layout grid base with the lightest fabrics toward the center and the darkest on the outer edges and with the bottom five rows using light green scraps and the top seven rows using off-white/tan scraps. *Note: The fabrics should gradually blend from light to dark giving the look of a watercolor, impressionist painting. The light center provides a nice contrast to the appliqué shapes.*

Step 5. When all squares are placed in a pleasing arrangement and there are none that stand out, set the iron on the wool setting with steam; fuse fabrics to the base. *Note: Do not glide the iron, but put it straight down and lift it up to move to the next area.*

Step 6. Fold the base right sides together along the first vertical grid line and stitch a seam ¼" in from the fold line down the entire length as shown in Figure 1. In the same manner, stitch along each vertical grid line in sequence. *Note: It is helpful to alternate the direction of the stitching to keep the base completely straight.*

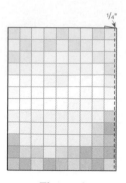

Figure 1
Fold the base on the back along the first vertical grid line and stitch a seam ¼" in from the fold line down the entire length.

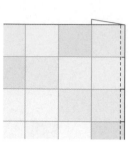

Figure 2
Clip seams at intersections just to stitching line.

Step 7. Clip seams on lines at each intersection of squares, clipping just to stitching as shown in Figure 2. From the back, press all seams in one direction.

Step 8. Stitch along the horizontal grid lines as in Step 6; clip and press as in Step 7. Press the front side.

Step 9. Cut two 2½" x 19½" A strips and two 2½" x 18½" B strips black print. Sew the B strips to opposite long sides and the A strips to the top and bottom of the pieced center; press seams toward strips.

Appliqué

Step 1. Prepare templates using patterns given. *Note: Pattern is already reversed for fusible appliqué.*

Step 2. Trace appliqué shapes onto the paper side of the fusible web referring to pattern for color. Trace 15 grape shapes.

Step 3. Cut out shapes, leaving a margin around each one; fuse shapes to the wrong side of the fabric scraps referring to full-size pattern for color. Fuse grape shapes on the wrong side of purple scrap.

Step 4. Cut out shapes on traced lines; remove paper backing.

Step 5. Begin by pinning basket shape to the background aligning basket bottom three rows up from the bottom edge and leaving basket top open to insert fruit pieces. Pin remaining pieces on background in numerical order; fuse in place. Fuse basket and then leaf and grapes that are layered on the basket.

Fruit Bowl Watercolor
Placement Diagram
19" x 22"

Step 6. Draw stems on apples and pears and mark lines in pineapple leaf using the brown fine-point fabric marker and referring to pattern for positioning.

Finishing

Step 1. Sandwich batting between the completed top and prepared backing piece; pin or baste layers together to hold flat for quilting.

Step 2. Quilt as desired by hand or machine. *Note: The sample shown was not quilted.*

Step 3. When quilting is complete, trim batting and backing even with quilted top; remove pins or basting.

Step 4. Cut three 2¼" by fabric width strips black print. Join strips on short ends to make one long strip for binding.

Step 5. Fold the binding strip in half along length with wrong sides together; press.

Step 6. Bind edges referring to the General Instructions. ❖

Fruit Bowl Motif

Basket of Flowers

By Marian Shenk

Shadow appliqué results in a soft, smooth look in this basket of fabric flowers.

Shadow Appliqué

This technique does not require any appliqué stitches. The basted appliqué motifs are covered with voile.
The shapes are outlined-stitched along edges and details are added with embroidery stitches.

Project Specifications

Skill Level: Beginner
Framed Size: 14" x 14"

Materials

- 18" x 18" square white-on-white print
- 18" x 18" square white voile
- Scrap dark purple solid for flower petals
- 9" x 9" square green solid for leaves and bud ends
- 8" x 8" square yellow solid for bow and flower centers
- 1 fat quarter bright orchid solid for flowers and buds
- ¼ yard brown print for basket and handle
- Backing 16" x 16"
- Purple, brown, green and yellow 6-strand embroidery floss
- 1 yard gold lamé Clover Quick Bias
- 14"-square gold frame
- 14" x 14" square cardboard

- Fabric glue stick
- UHU liquid-glue pen
- Basic sewing tools and supplies and brown paper bag

Appliqué

Step 1. Prepare templates for appliqué shapes using full-size pattern given. Cut as follows: three bright orchid flowers, 14 green leaves, eight bright orchid buds, eight green bud ends, three yellow flower centers, yellow bow pieces, one brown print basket and handle and six dark purple flower petals (reverse three).

Step 2. Fold the white-on-white print background piece and crease to mark centers.

Step 3. Center and arrange the basket and handle pieces 2⅝" from bottom edge of the background in numerical order referring to the full-size pattern. When satisfied with placement, use the fabric glue stick to hold the basket piece in place.

Step 4. Tuck the two center leaves under the edge of the basket and glue in place.

Step 5. Cut gold lamé quick bias pieces for basket using full-size pattern pieces 4–8 from full-size pattern; fuse the gold lamé quick bias pieces in place on the basket in numerical order.

Step 6. Arrange remaining appliqué shapes in place on top of and above basket referring to the full-size pattern and the Placement Diagram for positioning. When satisfied with arrangement, use the fabric glue stick to hold pieces in place.

Step 7. Place the 18" x 18" square white voile on top of glued motif; pin carefully to avoid leaving pin holes in the voile.

Step 8. Using 2 strands of embroidery floss to match fabrics, straight-stitch through voile, glued shapes and background to create quilt-like stitches.

Basket of Flowers

Step 9. Add stem details using 2 strands green embroidery floss and a stem stitch. Add bud details using 2 strands purple embroidery floss and long straight stitches.

Step 10. Center the completed design on the cardboard square; use fabric glue stick to secure in several places under the applied motifs.

Step 11. Turn the piece over and place a line of liquid glue around edges of cardboard's backside.

Step 12. Pull the excess fabric to the backside and press onto the glued cardboard; let dry.

Step 13. Cut a 14" x 14" square of brown paper bag; glue to the cardboard using liquid-glue pen to cover raw edges.

Step 14. Insert completed piece inside the purchased frame and secure. ❖

Basket of Flowers
Placement Diagram
14" x 14"

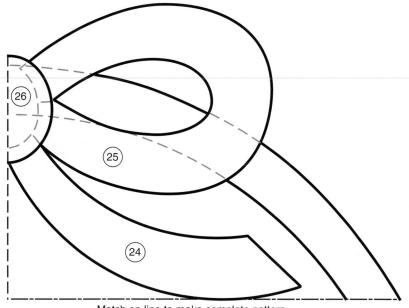

Match on line to make complete pattern.

Match on line to make complete pattern

Center

Place line on fold

Basket of Flowers Motif

Floral Denim Bag

By Marian Shenk

Silk flowers create the appliqués that are stitched to the flap of this casual, yet elegant purse.

Silk Flower Appliqué

Choose different-size silk flowers that when taken apart will lie flat. Use a bit of fabric glue to secure and stitch in place using nylon tulle to create a shadow effect.

Floral Denim Bag
Placement Diagram
Approximately 14" x 10"

Project Specifications

Skill Level: Intermediate
Purse Size: Approximately 14" x 10"

Materials

- ¼ yard blue nylon tulle
- ½ yard light blue denim
- ½ yard lining to match
- All-purpose thread to match denim
- Clear nylon monofilament
- ½ yard heavyweight interfacing
- 1 hook-and-loop fastener
- 1 stem green silk leaves with different-size leaves
- 8 small purple, four medium white and one large lavender silk flower that when taken apart will lie flat
- Purple 6-strand embroidery floss
- 1 (¾") purple button
- 3 purple and 8 blue ⅜" buttons
- Fabric glue stick
- Basic sewing tools and supplies

Instructions

Step 1. Prepare a template for flap and gusset using pattern pieces given; cut as directed on each piece.

Step 2. Baste the interfacing to the wrong side of one flap piece.

Step 3. Take the silk flowers and leaves apart and hand-press flat.

Step 4. Arrange the leaves (sample uses 13) and flowers on the flap piece referring to the Placement Diagram for positioning and overlapping as necessary. When satisfied with positioning, secure in place with a few dabs of fabric glue on each piece.

Step 5. Lay the blue nylon tulle flap piece over the fabric flap. Using clear nylon monofilament in the top of the machine and all-purpose thread in the bobbin, stitch around each flower and leaf shapes to secure.

Step 6. Make three straight stitches on each petal of the medium flowers using 2 strands purple embroidery floss. Sew buttons to the flap to make flower centers referring to the Placement Diagram and project photo for positioning.

Step 7. Place the remaining fabric flap right sides together with the front flap; stitch around curved edges. Turn right side out; press to make a smooth curve.

Step 8. Baste the top opening of the flap closed.

Step 9. Cut a 14½" x 20½" rectangle each light blue denim, heavyweight interfacing and lining.

Step 10. Transfer dart lines to all gusset pieces; stitch darts as shown in Figure 1. Trim and press darts open to reduce bulk as shown in Figure 2.

Step 11. Pin fabric gusset pieces to the long sides of the

Figure 1
Stitch darts on gusset pieces as shown.

fabric rectangle as shown in Figure 3; stitch. Repeat for lining and interfacing layers.

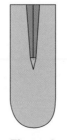

Figure 2
Trim and press darts open to reduce bulk.

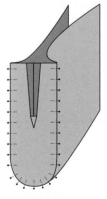

Figure 3
Pin fabric gusset pieces to the long sides of the fabric rectangle.

Step 12. Pin the flap piece right sides together with one 14½" edge of the stitched bag body; baste to hold.

Floral Denim Bag

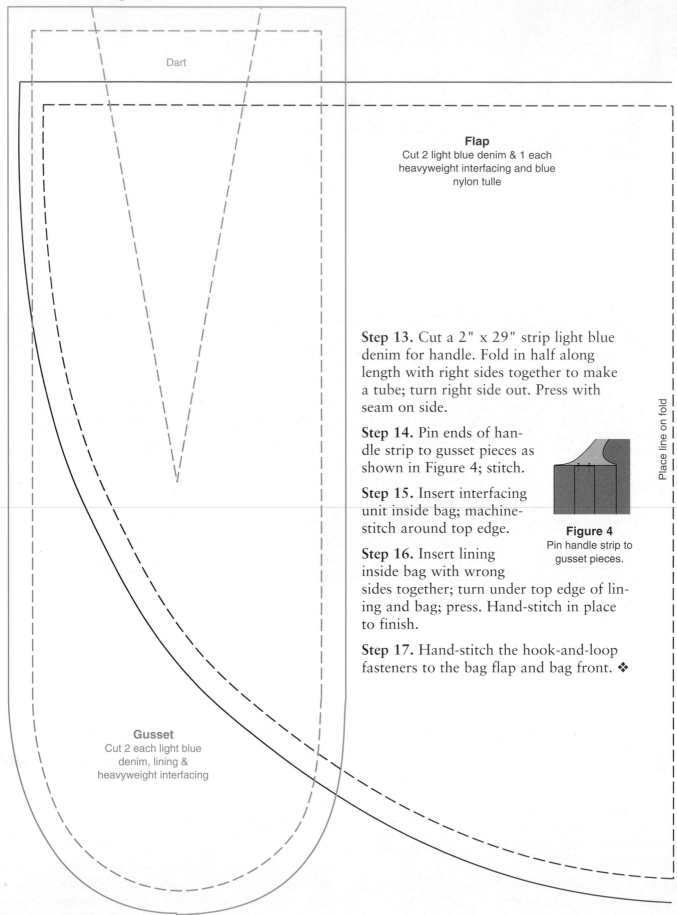

Dart

Flap
Cut 2 light blue denim & 1 each
heavyweight interfacing and blue
nylon tulle

Gusset
Cut 2 each light blue
denim, lining &
heavyweight interfacing

Place line on fold

Step 13. Cut a 2" x 29" strip light blue denim for handle. Fold in half along length with right sides together to make a tube; turn right side out. Press with seam on side.

Step 14. Pin ends of handle strip to gusset pieces as shown in Figure 4; stitch.

Step 15. Insert interfacing unit inside bag; machine-stitch around top edge.

Figure 4
Pin handle strip to
gusset pieces.

Step 16. Insert lining inside bag with wrong sides together; turn under top edge of lining and bag; press. Hand-stitch in place to finish.

Step 17. Hand-stitch the hook-and-loop fasteners to the bag flap and bag front. ❖

Undersea Stained Glass

By Judith Sandstrom

Bright tone-on-tones provide the perfect contrast for the black narrow bias tape in this stained glass–style wall quilt.

Leadline Tape in Stained Glass Technique

Use ³⁄₁₆"-wide black leadline tape to eliminate the need to create your own bias strips for use in covering edges of pieces in this stained glass technique.

Project Specifications

Skill Level: Beginner
Quilt Size: 20¼" x 23"

Materials

- ⅛–¼ yard or scraps blue, green, gold, aqua, peach and gray prints or tone-on-tones
- ¼ yard blue print for border
- ⅓ yard coral tone-on-tone for appliqué and binding
- ¾ yard white tone-on-tone for background and backing
- Batting 25" x 27"
- 2.0 twin needle
- Black and white all-purpose thread
- 1 yard Wonder-Under fusible web
- 11¼ yards ³⁄₁₆"-wide black rayon leadline tape
- Aleene's tacky fabric glue
- Basic sewing tools and supplies, and erasable fabric marker or pencil

Appliqué

Step 1. Prewash and iron all fabrics before cutting.

Step 2. From white tone-on-tone print, cut a 15¾" x 18½" rectangle for background and a 25" x 27" rectangle for backing; set backing piece aside. Fold background piece in quarters and crease to mark the center.

Step 3. Prepare templates for pattern pieces using the pattern given for one-quarter of the full-size design. Arrange templates by color.

Step 4. Place templates right side down on the paper side of the fusible web; trace as directed on the pattern for number to cut, keeping the same color pieces together in sections. Reverse pieces as directed on patterns.

Step 5. Cut pieces apart in sections, leaving a margin around each section. Fuse sections to the wrong side of fabrics as directed on patterns for color. Cut out shapes on traced lines; remove paper backing.

Step 6. Copy the whole one-quarter pattern on paper. Center the pattern on the wrong side of the background; pin to hold. Tape to a window or use a light box and transfer the complete design to the background, moving the paper pattern to other quarters of the background when finished with one area and using an erasable fabric marker or pencil.

Step 7. Arrange and pin shapes on the marked background referring to the marked lines, pattern and Placement Diagram for positioning. *Note: Pieces will be touching but not overlapping, except where marked on pattern. There should be a ¼" seam allowance on the background outer edges.*

Step 8. When satisfied with placement, fuse shapes in place referring to manufacturer's instructions.

Step 9. Referring to the full-size one-quarter pattern for application order and to Using Leadline Tape, cover all edges of fused appliqué shapes with the ³⁄₁₆"-wide black leadline tape.

Completing the Top

Step 1. Cut two strips each 3" x 18½" and 3" x 20¾" blue print.

Step 2. Sew the shorter strips to opposite long sides and the longer strips to the top and bottom of the appliquéd center; press seams toward strips.

Finishing

Step 1. Sandwich batting between the completed top and prepared backing piece; pin or baste layers together to hold flat for quilting.

Step 2. Stitch leadline tape edges to act as quilting referring to Using Leadline Tape. *Note: The leadline tape ends extend into the seam allowance area to be stitched into the border seam allowance on some edge pieces.*

Step 3. Machine-stitch in ditch of border seams using white all-purpose thread.

Step 4. When quilting is complete, trim batting and backing even with quilted top; remove pins or basting.

Step 5. Cut three 2¼" by fabric width strips coral tone-on-tone. Join strips on short ends to make one long strip for binding.

Step 6. Fold the binding strip in half along length with wrong sides together; press.

Step 7. Bind edges referring to the General Instructions.

Using Leadline Tape

Leadline tape has some advantages over fabric bias tape and is easy to use. Refer to the following hints when applying to project.

Step 1. Stretch the tape around curved edges.

Step 2. Manufacturer suggests searing ends with a match to prevent fraying, but in the project the ends are secured with tacky fabric glue.

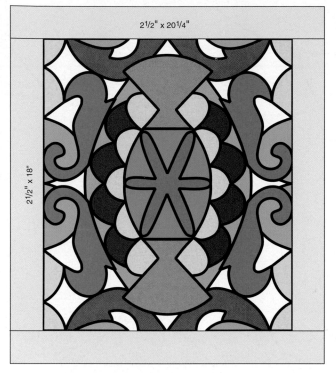

Undersea Stained Glass
Placement Diagram
20¼" x 23"

slightly over the edge of the appliqué shape as shown in Figure 2.

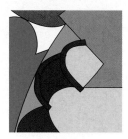

Figure 2
Cut the tape at the end so it will extend slightly over the edge of the appliqué shape.

Figure 3
Cover the ends with the next piece of tape.

Step 6. Start with smaller pieces and cover the ends with the next piece of tape as shown in Figure 3.

Step 7. Use a continuous piece of tape when possible in order to have fewer ends to cover.

Step 8. Points may be continued in one piece by folding the tape over itself as shown in Figure 4.

Figure 4
Points may be continued in 1 piece by folding the tape over itself.

Step 9. Work from the center out or refer to pattern for number order.

Step 10. Ends at edges should extend into seam allowance to be included in border seams.

Step 11. Stitch on both sides of the tape using black all-purpose thread and starting in the center and working toward the outside.

Step 12. A 2.0 twin needle may be used to stitch both edges at the same time. Use a continuous stitch whenever possible to avoid starts and stops. ❖

Step 3. Center the tape over the edge of the fabric to be outlined as shown in Figure 1.

Step 4. Apply tacky fabric glue to the edge of the appliqué shape; center the tape over the appliqué edge and press flat. Continue adding glue as you place the tape along the edge.

Step 5. Cut the tape at the end so it will extend

Figure 1
Center the tape over the edge of the fabric to be outlined.

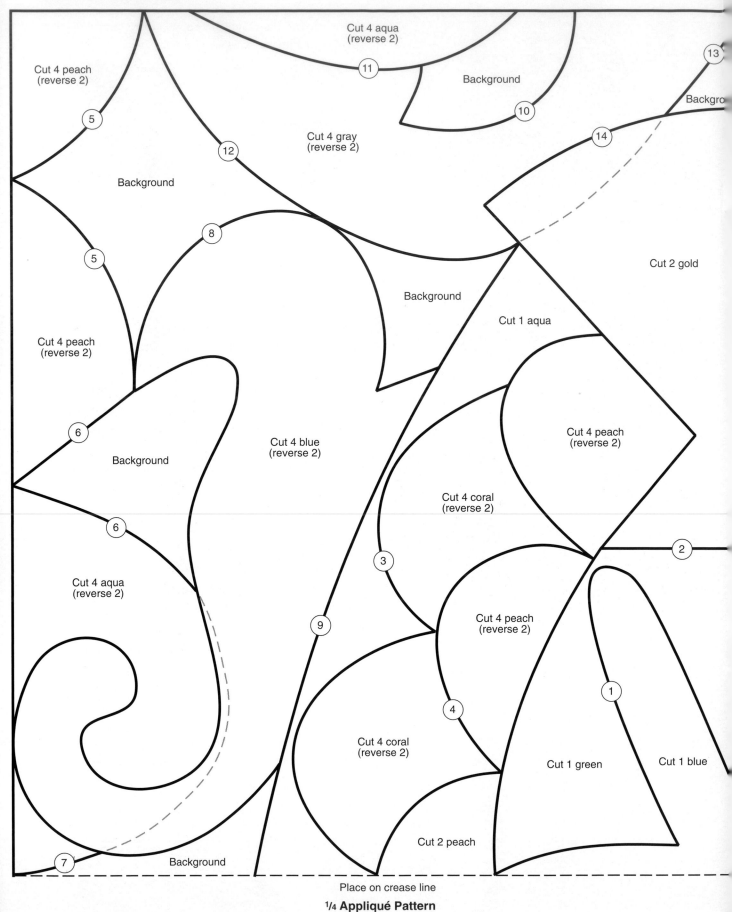

Cut 4 aqua
(reverse 2)

⑪

Background

⑩

⑬

Background

Cut 4 peach
(reverse 2)

⑤

⑫

Cut 4 gray
(reverse 2)

⑭

Background

Background

⑧

Cut 2 gold

Cut 1 aqua

⑤

Cut 4 peach
(reverse 2)

Background

Cut 4 peach
(reverse 2)

⑥

Background

Cut 4 blue
(reverse 2)

Cut 4 coral
(reverse 2)

⑥

②

Cut 4 aqua
(reverse 2)

③

Cut 4 peach
(reverse 2)

⑨

④

Cut 4 coral
(reverse 2)

①

Cut 1 green

Cut 1 blue

⑦

Background

Cut 2 peach

Place on crease line

¼ Appliqué Pattern

Folk-Art Tulips

By Julie Weaver

Wool felt makes a durable, simple-to-stitch project with a folk-art look.

Appliqué With Wool Felt

WoolFelt® from National Nonwovens creates a fleece-like effect when washed. Wet felt completely; squeeze by hand to remove as much moisture as possible. Dry in a standard clothes dryer on regular setting until felt is nearly dry; lay flat to finish drying. This process causes the felt to shrink somewhat. Sizes given allow for shrinkage. Because felt sticks to itself, appliqué projects can be completed using only a few pins to help hold the appliqué shapes in place while stitching. Hand-stitch around shapes using pearl cotton and a blanket stitch to secure. Use a large sharp needle to make long quilting stitches close to appliqué shapes to hold layers together.

Project Specifications

Skill Level: Beginner
Quilt Size: 20" x 32"

Materials

- 8" x 8" square plum wool felt
- 12" x 12" square each green, dark gray and rose wool felt
- ⅓ yard burgundy wool felt
- ½ yard light gray wool felt
- 1⅓ yards black wool felt
- Thin batting 19" x 31"

- 2 balls No. 8 black pearl cotton
- Basic sewing tools and supplies and large sharp needle

Instructions

Step 1. Wash the wool felt referring to Appliqué With Wool Felt.

Step 2. Cut two 20" x 32" rectangles black wool felt; set aside one for backing.

Step 3. Cut one 14" x 24" rectangle light gray wool felt for center background. Place on one 20" x 32" rectangle black felt approximately 4" from the top and bottom and 3" from each side; pin in place.

Step 4. Referring to Figure 1 and using 2 strands black pearl cotton and evenly spaced, ⅜"-long blanket stitches, sew the light gray piece to the black background piece.

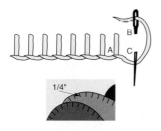

Figure 1
Blanket-stitch around edges
using 1/4" stitches as shown.

Step 5. Prepare templates for appliqué shapes using patterns given, extending pieces for overlapping as necessary. Cut pieces from wool felt as directed on each piece for color.

Step 6. Center the pot piece 1" from bottom edge of the light gray background piece; pin the pot rim and circles in place.

Step 7. Center large stem, tucking edge under pot rim; pin in place. Place ends of small and medium stems under pot rim referring to the

Folk-Art Tulips

placement lines on pot rim pattern.

Step 8. Stitch shapes in place as in Step 4.

Step 9. Arrange the remaining floral shapes referring to the Placement Diagram; pin and stitch in place as in Step 4.

Step 10. Beginning at top edge, arrange A pieces around the outer edge of the black background piece, overlapping each approximately ½" as shown in Figure 2 and placing five A pieces on the top and bottom and eight on each side.

Figure 2
Overlap A pieces
approximately ½".

Folk-Art Tulips
Placement Diagram
20" x 32"

Adjust as necessary to evenly space A pieces.

Step 11. Stitch curved edges of A pieces in place as in Step 4.

Step 12. Center the thin batting on the backing piece set aside in Step 2. *Note: Batting is ½" smaller all around than backing.* Place appliquéd top on the layers with edges even; trim if necessary.

Step 13. Using 1 strand black pearl cotton, sew large stitches around the entire appliquéd motif and around edges of A pieces to hold layers together.

Step 14. Attach front to back at edges as in Step 4. ❖

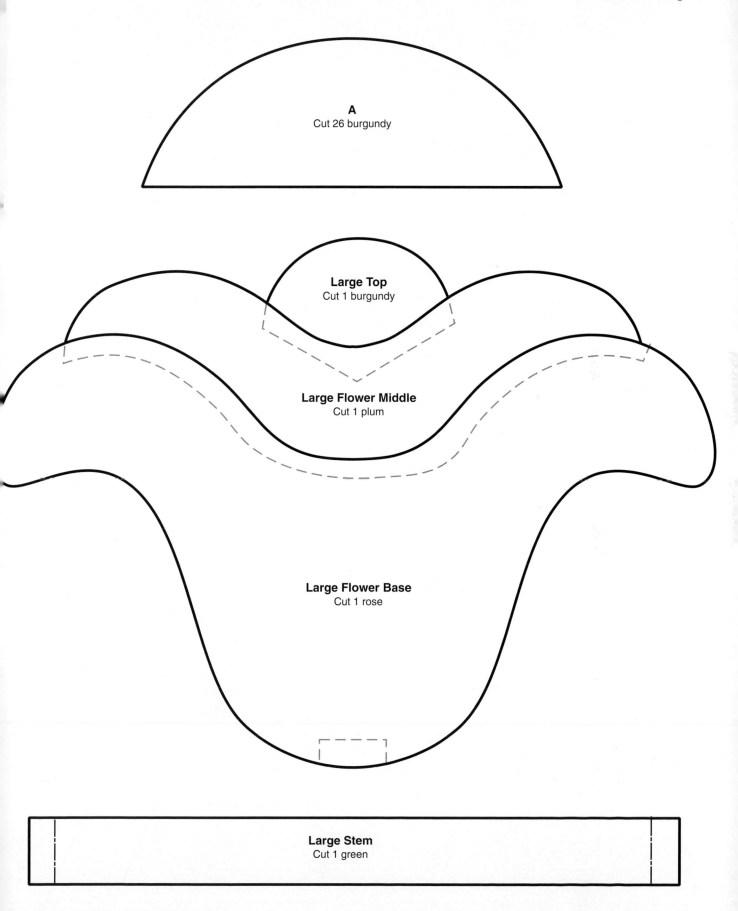

A
Cut 26 burgundy

Large Top
Cut 1 burgundy

Large Flower Middle
Cut 1 plum

Large Flower Base
Cut 1 rose

Large Stem
Cut 1 green

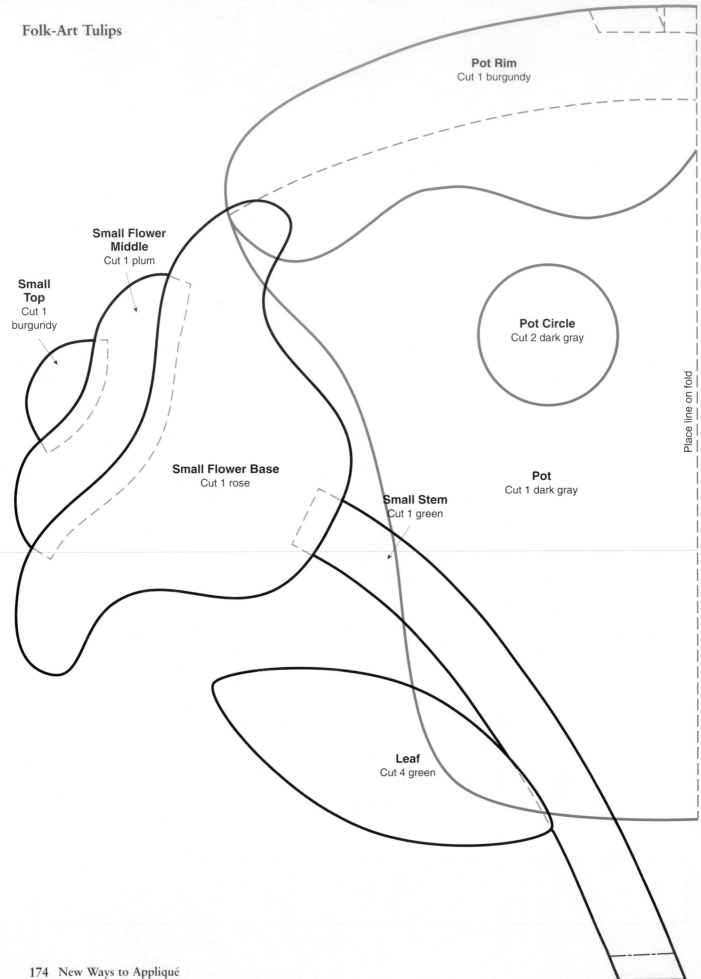

Pot Rim
Cut 1 burgundy

Small Flower
Middle
Cut 1 plum

Small
Top
Cut 1
burgundy

Pot Circle
Cut 2 dark gray

Small Flower Base
Cut 1 rose

Small Stem
Cut 1 green

Pot
Cut 1 dark gray

Place line on fold

Leaf
Cut 4 green

**Medium
Flower
Middle**
Cut 1 plum

Folk-Art Tulips

**Medium
Top**
Cut 1
burgundy

Medium Flower Base
Cut 1 rose

Medium Stem
Cut 1 green

Special Thanks

We would like to thank the talented quilt designers whose work is featured in this collection.

Mary Ayres
Zebra Kid's Quilt, 46

Barbara Clayton
Cardinal Christmas Stocking, 88

Holly Daniels
Full of Love, 148

Lucy A. Fazely & Michael L. Burns
Raggy Rainbow Quilt, 13

Sue Harvey
Lollipop Flowers, 22
No Snails in My Garden, 128
Wildflower Bouquet, 142

Connie Kauffman
Baby's Stars Quilt, 27
Christmas Outlines, 82
Pastel Hearts Baby Quilt, 42

Plants in My Window, 152

Sue Kruger
Twinkle, Twinkle Little Star, 30

Chris Malone
Loving Angel Pillow & Card, 78
Snowman Tree Skirt, 69
Berber Fleece Jacket, 136

Patsy Moreland
All That Jazz, 114

Connie Rand
Fall Fantasy, 118

Judith Sandstrom
Cartwheel Clowns, 38
Counting Sheep 109
Fruit Bowl Watercolor, 156
Patchwork Posies, 8
Undersea Stained Glass, 167

Carla Schwab
My Favorite Season Penny Rug, 133

Marian Shenk
Basket of Flowers, 160
Floral Denim Bag, 164
Signs of the Season, 74
Teddy & Friends Wall Quilt, 50

Ruth Swasey
Nodding Tulips, 123

Jodi Warner
Snow Star & Nine-Patch Lap
    Quilt, 104

Julie Weaver
Bunny Hugs, 17
Dresden Cabins, 100
Festive Holly Table Cover, 66
Folk-Art Tulips, 171
Holiday Kitchen Cheer, 58

Eileen Westfall
Holly Berry Noel Wreath, 94

Contact Information

The following companies provided fabric and/or supplies for projects in New Ways to Appliqué. If you are unable to locate a product locally, contact the manufacturers listed below for the closest retail or mail-order source in your area.

Beacon Adhesives
(914) 699-3400
www.beacon1.com

Clover
(800) 233-1703

Collins/Prym-Dritz Corp.
(800) 845-4948
www.dritz.com

Crafter's Pick
(800) 776-7616
www.crafterspick.com

DecoArt, Inc.
(800) 367-3047
www.decoart.com

Duncan Enterprises
(800) 438-6226
www.Duncan-Enterprises.com

Fabric Café
(903) 509-5999
www.fabriccafe.com

HTC-Handler Textile Corp.
(770) 938-7014
www.htc-handler.com

June Tailor
(800) 844-5400
www.junetailor.com

J. T. Trading Corp.
(203) 270-7744
www.sprayandfix.com

Pellon
(800) 223-5275
www.pellonideas.com

Sulky of America
(800) 874-4115

www.sulky.com

The Appliqué Pressing Sheet
Bear Thread Designs
(281) 462-0661
www.bearthreaddesigns.com

The Warm Company
(800) 234-9276
www.warmcompany.com

Therm O Web
(800) 323-0799
www.thermoweb.com

Wrights
(877) 597-4448
www.wrights.com

Fabrics & Supplies

Page 8: *Patchwork Posies*—HeatnBond Lite and ¼"-wide HeatnBond The Quilter's Edge Lite iron-on adhesives from Therm O Web, Hobbs Heirloom cotton batting, Wrights double-fold bias tape, DMC quilting thread and needles, and Fiskars rotary-cutting tools.

Page 13: *Raggy Rainbow Quilt*—Beacon's Liqui-Fuse liquid fusible web, Transition Flannels from Classic Cottons, Warm & Natural cotton batting from The Warm Co., Dual Duty Plus all-purpose thread, clear nylon monofilament and Star Multicolored Quilting and Craft Thread from Coats. The quilt was machine-pieced with a Bernina Artista 165.

Page 17: *Bunny Hugs*—Sulky KK 2000 Temporary Spray Adhesive, Steam-A-Seam 2 double stick fusible web from The Warm Co., and The Appliqué Pressing Sheet.

Page 22: *Lollipop Flowers*—Pellon Wonder-Under fusible web and Stitch-n-Tear fabric stabilizer, Chenille By The Inch; Chenille Brush and Chenille Cutting Guide from Fabric Café; and Sulky Rayon Thread.

Page 27: *Baby's Stars Quilt*—Sulky rayon thread, Sulky KK 2000 Temporary Spray Adhesive and Hobbs Heirloom Premium batting.

Page 30: *Twinkle, Twinkle Little Star*—DecoArt Americana acrylic paints and fabric painting medium, Sakura black Identi-Pen fine-point permanent marker and Teflon ironing sheet.

Page 38: *Cartwheel Clowns*—Pellon Wonder-Under fusible web, Hobbs Heirloom cotton batting,

Fiskars rotary-cutting tools, and Pigma pens.

Page 42: *Pastel Hearts Baby Quilt*—Sulky pastel variegated rayon thread and Hobbs Heirloom Fusible cotton batting.

Page 46: *Zebra Kid's Quilt*—HeatnBond Lite iron-on adhesive from Therm O Web.

Page 50: *Teddy & Friends Wall Quilt*—HeatnBond Lite iron-on adhesive from Therm O Web, Clover Quick Bias Tape and Unique Stitch fabric glue from Collins/Prym-Dritz Corp.

Page 58: *Holiday Kitchen Cheer*—Lite Steam-A-Seam 2 double stick fusible web from The Warm Co. and The Appliqué Pressing Sheet.

Page 66: *Festive Holly Table Cover*—Lite Steam-A-Seam 2 double stick fusible web from The Warm Co.

Page 69: *Snowman Tree Skirt*—Fabri-Tac Permanent Adhesive from Beacon Adhesives, and Warm & Natural cotton batting from The Warm Co.

Page 74: *Signs of the Season*—HeatnBond Lite fusible web from Therm O Web.

Page 78: *Loving Angel Pillow & Card*—HeatnBond Lite iron-on adhesive from Therm O Web.

Page 82: *Christmas Outlines*—Steam-A-Seam 2 transfer web from The Warm Co., Sulky KK 2000 Temporary Spray Adhesive, Sulky gold metallic thread and Hobbs Premium cotton batting.

Page 88: *Cardinal Christmas Stocking*—Quilter's Press Bars from Collins/Prym-Dritz Corp.

Page 94: *Holly Berry Noel Wreath*—Steam-A-Seam 2 double stick fusible web from The Warm Co. and Quilter's Fusible Batting from June Tailor Inc.

Page 109: *Counting Sheep*—DMC quilting thread and needles, Fiskars rotary-cutting equipment, Pellon Wonder-Under fusible web and Stitch-n-Tear fabric stabilizer and Hobbs Heirloom cotton batting.

Page 114: *All That Jazz*—Warm & Natural fusible fleece and Steam-A-Seam 2 double stick fusible web from The Warm Co., Clover fusible bias Art. No. 700 BGY, Scrapbooking Music die cuts No. 28009 PE101 and Putting on the Glitz Jewel Box Kit No. 4879 from Westrim Crafts, Blumenthal Lansing Primary Favorite Things #442 and High Five #32 buttons, Cool Cats fabric collection by Nana for the Balson Hercules Group, Crafter's Pick Ultimate Glue, Susan Bates Luxite bone rings and DMC pearl cotton.

Page 118: *Fall Fantasy*—Hobbs Heirloom cotton batting with scrim binder and HeatnBond fusible web from Therm O Web.

Page 128: *No Snails in My Garden*—Meadowz fabric line by Jan Mullen for Marcus Brothers, Mettler Silk-Finish thread from American & Efird, Sulky rayon thread, Pellon Stitch-n-Tear fabric stabilizer, Wrights rainbow painted jumbo rickrack, 505 Spray and Fix temporary adhesive spray, 606 Spray and Fix spray-on fusible web and DK5 adhesive spray cleaner from J. T. Trading Corp. and Bo-Nash Giant Non-Stick Ironing & Craft Sheet.

Page 136: *Berber Fleece Jacket*—Pellon No. 911FF fusible interfacing.

Page 142: *Wildflower Bouquet*—Upsy Daisy, Textures and Basics fabrics from Northcott, Fairfield Natural cotton batting, Mettler Silk-Finish thread and Signature machine-quilting thread from American & Efird, 505 Spray & Fix basting spray from J.T. Trading Corp., Pellon Wonder-Under fusible web and Stitch-n-Tear fabric stabilizer, and Clover ¼" fusible bias maker and ¼"-wide fusible web.

Page 152: *Plants in My Window*—Hobbs Premium cotton batting, Sulky KK 2000 Temporary Spray Adhesive and Aleene's Tacky Easy Flow glue from Duncan Enterprises.

Page 156: *Fruit Bowl Watercolor*—Pellon Wonder-Under fusible web and Quilt Fuse from htc.

Page 160: *Basket of Flowers*—UHU liquid-glue pen and Clover Quick Bias Tape.

Page 167: *Undersea Stained Glass*—black leadline tape from Europa Imports Style No. 6671-0 (available at Jo-Ann Fabrics and Crafts or DianaSews@aol.com), Wonder-Under fusible web from Pellon, Hobbs Heirloom cotton batting and Aleene's Easy Flow Tacky Glue.

Page 171: *Folk-Art Tulips*—WoolFelt from National Nonwovens in the following colors: black, cobblestone, smoldering cinder, burgundy, Victorian rose, cypress garden and English rose.